An Ode to Mathematics
With Study Tips That Really Work!
Copyright © 2018
Michael J. Humphrey

$$ax^2 + bx + c = 0$$

$$x = \frac{-b \pm \sqrt{b^2 - 4ac}}{2a}$$

$$\frac{L}{1-L}$$

$$f(x)$$

$$\sum_{n=1}^{10} x^2$$

$$\frac{d}{dx}$$

$$\int_a^b F(x)\,dx$$

$$y = mx + b$$

Table of Contents

Introduction

While growing up in Saint Paul, Minnesota, my focus was rarely on anything academic. As a high school senior in 1982, I dropped out, and after a year of no direction, or opportunities, I reenrolled at Saint Paul Central High School, where I graduated at the bottom of my class in 1983. Yes, out of over 400 students, my class rank was 6th or 7th from the bottom.

The following year, I attended the University of Minnesota, General College (GC). GC was a college within the University of Minnesota network. Its focus was to provide scaffolding services for less traditional students who needed extra support. My first course was called the "College Survival Seminar," a class that provided many proven study habits and skills necessary for college. The study methods made a huge difference, and for the first time in my life, I was earning A's in difficult classes.

It was really a strange feeling going through college with good grades after struggling so badly in high school. For the first year of college, I would keep a copy of my grade report neatly folded in my wallet. Now and then, I would pull it out to reflect, sometimes in disbelief.

High school should be a place where students develop their strengths, and gain confidence in their capabilities, but unfortunately for many of us, we leave high school with a comprehensive list of the things we are incapable of doing. Math is a perfect example of a subject that many high school graduates feel they are no good at. The problem with this is that many will go on to pick careers, not based on what they like to do, but rather how much math is required for the training. If you would have asked me when I graduated if I was good at math, I would have thought you were crazy; but now here I am a high school math teacher. So just remember, your incapabilities are simply capabilities that you have not yet realized.

After attending the General College for two years, I enlisted into the United States Army where I served four years active and six years in the National Guard Reserve. After getting back from active duty service, I enrolled into the University of Minnesota's Institute of Technology where I received a Bachelor of Science in Mathematics. After working several jobs in the insurance and restaurant industry, I enrolled into the University of Minnesota's College of Education, where I spent two years obtaining teaching credentials.

Later, I got a job working for Saint Paul Schools' American Indian Education program, a federally funded program through the Indian Education Act of 1972. Cultural enrichment was a strong tenet of the program, so my time with the program was an enjoyable one I'll never forget. Several years later, a math teaching position opened up at Saint Paul Central High School, where I have been working ever since.

Two years ago, I started writing poems to go along with my math lessons. It was a lot of fun, so I made an earlier edition math poetry book called "Mr. Humphrey's Book of Math Poetry." This is my second math poetry book. I'm hoping that with my experience, this year's poems will be an improvement over the last. But what I am really excited about are the study tips – 29 of them – study tips that have made a huge difference for me. The power of these study tips, for those who apply them, is incredible. Over time, your grades will continue to get better if you use them.

If you want good grades, this is what you do
Find a good friend that wants them, too
We do it all the time in other areas of life
Athletics, work, or just getting through strife
The parts add up to more than a whole
Working synergistically as a group, I was told
So get together and show your support
Iron sharpens Iron when we finalize reports
Don't forget to schedule some fun
To reward yourself when the race is won
Catch a movie, or an outdoor activity
Your favorite food, yes, enjoy so happily
Because soon life's circle comes around
The journey continues in the race upward bound

Uses for this Book

- It's fun: For those who have taken high school math, some of the concepts from the poems may bring back memories. My intention is that the poetry is both informative and fun.

- It's a resource: The 29 study tips are a tremendous resource for students who want to improve their learning and get better grades.

- It's a lesson icebreaker for teachers: Just find a poem related to any lesson that you teach, and read it as an icebreaker to start class. Just remember to rehearse it a couple times to get the proper flow.

- Use it to connect: Literacy and English teachers could use the book to connect mathematical concepts, vocabulary, and terms across the curriculum.

- Classroom lessons: A study skills teacher could use the 29 study tips and make classroom lessons out of them. Students would read the book, and classroom discussions can be generated by the study tips.

About the 29 Study Tips

Think about two different groups of students with the following mindsets towards school:

Group A only cares about their GPAs, even to the exclusion of understanding or remembering later. As long as they get the grade, they don't care.

Group B wants to understand, learn and get involved. Participation in discussions and class activities are seen as opportunities for Group B students to deepen their knowledge.

Did you know that Group B students are going to have an overall higher average GPA? Also, Group B students will make it to higher academic levels than Group A. Just remember, if your goal is good grades, you may find a way to get them, sometimes without really learning; but if your focus is on learning, the grades take care of themselves.

DON'T WORRY ABOUT GRADES, FOCUS ON LEARNING, AND THE GRADES TAKE CARE OF THEMSELVES

Use the 29 study tips and focus on the learning!

An Ode to Mathematics

Oh mathematics, the universal code
So complex, so beautiful, to you we give ode

Musical, yet elemental, the key that unlocks
Galaxies, heavenly bodies, the time of the clock

In nature and art, so beautifully symmetric
A shout to mathematics so true and eclectic

Patterns, fractals, chaos, entropy
Order within disorder if you look so carefully

So intricately complex, you hide
throughout
To the creator's glory, forever searched out

From the stars of the heavens to
the galaxies
Speaking your language is like
music for me

Oh mathematics we shout
with glee

We give
an ode of respect to thee

An Ode to Mathematics

Math Poetry

Math is the language of the universe

Access to higher level thought

The key to understanding everything

Hope for all through rational reasoning

People everywhere love poetry

Options considered and mathematically deducted

Every day we use math, believe it or not

Truly worth the effort to follow the math trail

Reflect poetically

You are the Math

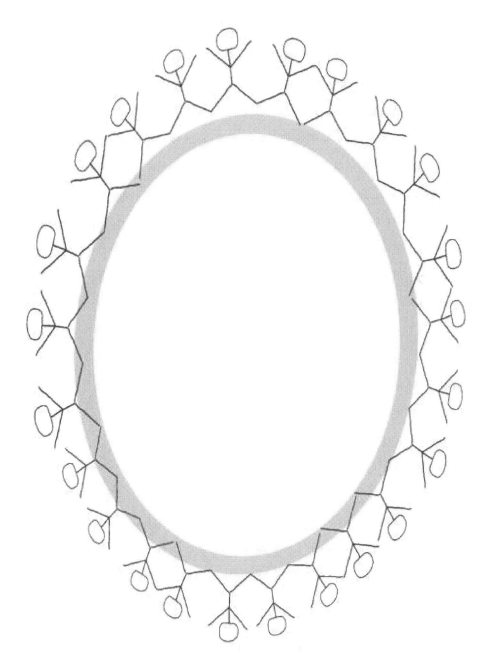

The World United Through Math Poetry

First Day Back

Summer's over and now you're here
It's the opening day of the school year

A time for pencils and big textbooks
Vacation is over, no sad looks

Just yesterday you slept on through
Now confined in school till two

But please don't fear, I must be clear
Follow the rules to have a good year

Remember your teachers care for you
Rules are given to help you through

Be kind, cooperative, and do your work
Impress your peers, contribute your worth

Do your homework every day
To greatly help your GPA

Your friends will think you're very smart
Showing your talent and doing your part

So set your goals and let's get straight
Enjoy your school year, let's make it great

Balancing = Equations

An equation solved, the variable's secluded
    All by itself, its value included
        The method is simple,
        let me explain
        A balanced approach
        in the next quatrain
        We add, subtract multiply, or divide
        By the same number
        on both sides`

        A balancing act,
        Yes, indeed
        Solving equations
        by the count of three
        Opposites cancel
        eliminating terms
        An isolated variable
        is our main concern
    All by itself, to one side of the equation
With answer in sight, just short of amazing

$$3x + 12 = 7x + 60$$

Think of a balance scale. Two expressions that are equal, would be the same on both sides of a balance scale. So think of the equal sign as the balancing point of the scale.

$$3x + 12 = 7x + 60$$
$$-7x \qquad -7x$$
$$\overline{}$$
$$-4x + 12 = 0 + 60$$

$$-4x + 12 = 60$$
$$ -12 \quad -12$$
$$\overline{}$$
$$-4x + 0 = 48$$

If you have a scale that is already balanced, then it will remain balanced if you change both sides in the same way.

$$\frac{-4x}{-4} = \frac{48}{-4}$$

$$\boxed{X = -12}$$

Balancing means to perform the same operations on both sides of the equal sign. The goal of balancing is to isolate the variable to one side of the equal sign in order to find its solution.

21

Clearing Fractions in Equations

Solving equations with fractions involved
Just clear them out and reach for the clouds
　　Factor denominators to find LCM
　　　　Of the denominators
　　　　to eliminate them
　　　　Each prime factor's
　　　　highest power
　　　　Made into a product
　　　　the LCM will flower
　　　　The least common multiple multiplied to both
　　　　sides
　　　　Watch what happens
　　　　when the denominators
　　　　　　collide
　　　　They cancel out those
　　　　dirty denominators
　　Common factors are out, we'll see you later
　You now have an equation cleared of fractions
Let's get solving, it's time for action

$$\frac{-3}{X-7} + \frac{4x}{7} = \frac{21+20X}{35}$$

$$LCM = 35(X-7)$$

$$35(X-7)\left[\frac{-3}{X-7} + \frac{4x}{7} = \frac{21+20X}{35}\right]$$

$$35(X-7) \cdot \frac{-3}{X-7} + \overset{5}{35}(X-7) \frac{4x}{7} = 35(X-7) \cdot \frac{21+20X}{35}$$

$$-105 + 20X(X-7) = (X-7)(21+20X)$$

$$-105 + 20X^2 - 140X = 20X^2 - 119X - 147$$
$$\underline{-20X^2 \qquad \Big/ \quad -20X^2}$$
$$-105 - 140X = -119X - 147$$
$$\underline{+119X \qquad \Big/ \quad +119X}$$
$$-105 - 21X = -147$$
$$\underline{+105 \qquad \Big/ \quad +105}$$
$$-21X = -42$$
$$\boxed{X = 2}$$

23

Rational Equations

An equation that contains a rational expression
Rational equations are the next lesson

Just clear the fractions, look and see
Multiply everything by the LCD!

The fractions cancel totally
Now solve the equation naturally

Next, check the solution for zero denominators
Extraneous solutions, we kick them
out of here

Rational equations are really
rational
Now think really big, cause
we're going national

Ratios and Proportions

A quotient of numbers **a** and **b**
Form a ratio, as you can see

Proportions are formed with two ratios equal
Next we solve them for the next sequel

a is to **b** as **c** is to **d**
Solving proportions will set you free

Cross-multiply and divide is how you solve
Break out your pencil and get involved

The unknown value will come to you
You solved the proportion and now you're through

A farmer mixes his cattle feed, 3 parts corn for every 7 parts grass.
How much grass will be needed if the farmer has 12 bushels of corn?

Answer: Just set up a ratio of corn to grass.
Then, set up an equation using proportions

$$\frac{Corn}{grass} = \frac{3}{7} = \frac{12}{x}$$

$$\frac{3x}{3} = \frac{\overset{4}{\cancel{12}}(7)}{3}$$

$$x = 28 \text{ bushels of grass}$$

Happy Birthday!

A very special day of the calendar year
Another year older, let's celebrate and cheer

Happy birthday! Happy birthday! We call it out
Another year older, a reason to shout

Family, friends and classmates everywhere
Treated so special by those who really care

Cakes, candles and birthday wishes
Blow them out; then do the dishes

Study Tip 1: Set Academic Goals

It was once written, some thousands of years ago, "A man without a goal is a spiritually dead man." I don't know the exact origination of this quote. My grandmother told me this when I was a child. But if we look at what this means in today's context, it may sound something like this: "A person without a goal cannot be motivated." Think of an athlete who endures brutal workout and practice routines. An athlete knows that they must endure many hardships to achieve what they want; so, too, does a successful student know that goals must be set. Those who set goals have higher average GPAs than their counterparts.

Set daily, weekly, monthly, quarterly, yearly and long-term academic goals. Then mentally prepare yourself for the hard work and sacrifice that it will take. Your goals can range from the simple daily, to the more thought-out, long-term ones.

Daily, Weekly, Quarterly, Yearly, and-Long-Term Goals

- Daily goals are certain things that must be accomplished daily, and they should line up with some long-term objective.
- The purpose of the weekly review is to summarize, reflect, and revisit the learning objectives of the week prior.
- Periodic or Quarterly reviews are more extensive weekly reviews, except you cover all the objectives for a particular period of time, usually done for test or quiz review.
- For yearly goals, one must think of what really needs to be accomplished in order to makes strides towards the long-term objective.
- A long-term goals are things like career fields, marriage and family makeup, financial status, retirement, etc.

Daily Goal Example:

- Attend every class on time and pay attention to all instructions. (Note: if you use your phone for anything other than classroom purposes, you violate this one.)
- Ask questions for clarification.
- Listen to everyone else's questions.
- Participate to your fullest at every chance.
- Start all homework immediately after the lesson, or at the earliest possible opportunity. Math homework should be worked on first, since the concepts are more easily forgotten.

Weekly Goal Example:

- Review lessons, homework, notes, old quizzes or tests from each class (especially math class).
- Get caught up on all homework and assignments from all classes.

Systems of Linear Equations

Equations lined up with multiple variables
Systems of equations will rock in stereo

We find out where the cost is equal
Or where we meet for the next sequel

When all the equations lined up are linear
A Linear System could never be prettier

Solved through quite a variety of techniques
Graphically, algebraically and substituting

So write your equations and get involved
This Linear System will be solved

$$3x - 2y = 15$$
$$7x + 2y = 25$$

Solving Systems using Tables or Graphs

A solution point for a linear system
Solves them both when you substitute in them

For each equation, make an x-y table
Solutions match, as seen on cable

Graph the lines, another way to do it
The point of intersection is the solution through it

So graph those lines and complete those tables
A linear system's solution's enabled

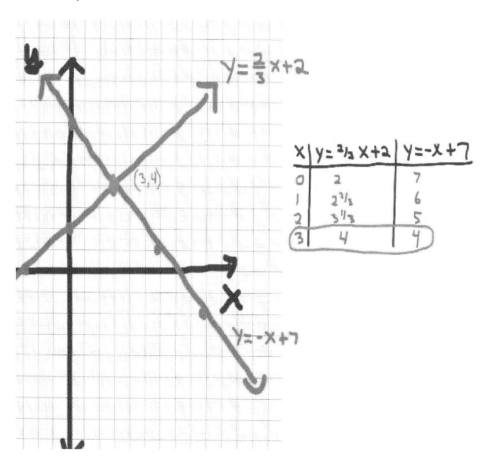

$y = \frac{2}{3}x + 2$

$y = -x + 7$

(3,4)

X	$y = \frac{2}{3}X + 2$	$Y = -X + 7$
0	2	7
1	$2\frac{2}{3}$	6
2	$3\frac{1}{3}$	5
3	4	4

Solving Using Calculator Display

Systems solved through graphs and tables
Use a computer that's graphically enabled

Intersection point is a solution, too
Linear systems are solved for you

When table values of functions match
You get the solution and that's a fact

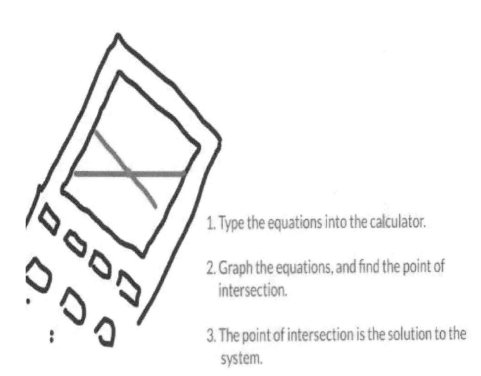

1. Type the equations into the calculator.

2. Graph the equations, and find the point of intersection.

3. The point of intersection is the solution to the system.

Substitution Method

System of equations, solved in many ways
Substitution method is what we learn today

Just solve for a variable, it doesn't matter which
Substitute to other equation as it fits

Equation it now has only one variable
Solved many times in previous scenarios

Don't forget to substitute back
To find the other value and stay on track

$$2x + y = 7$$
$$3x - y = 3$$

Notice that either of the two equations can be solved for y. In this example, I solved for y in the second equation.

$$y = 3x - 3$$

Now, we substitute what y equals in the second equation, into the y variable of the first equation.

$$2x + (3x - 3) = 7$$

Now we have an equation with one variable x which can be solved for. Once we solve for x, back substitute to find y.

$$2x + 3x - 3 = 7$$
$$5x = 10$$
$$x = 2$$

$$y = 3(2) - 3 = 3$$

$$(2,3)$$

Final solution in ordered pair form.

Solved by Elimination

Equations combined, variables eliminated
Solution point found of the system insinuated

Multiples of equations summed together
Eliminating variables to one less letter

When you get down to an equation of one
Time to solve and have some fun

Don't forget your back substitution
To find the other variable's solution

$$2x + y = 7$$
$$3x - y = 3$$

Multiples of one equation can be added to another equation, usually with the purpose of eliminating variables. In this example, if we simply add the equations together, the y variable drops out.

$$5x + 0 = 10$$
$$5x = 10$$
$$\boxed{x = 2}$$

$$2(2) + y = 7$$

Substituting into equation 1

$$4 + y = 7$$
$$\boxed{y = 3}$$

$$\boxed{(2,3)}$$

Study Tip 2: Be Aware of Your Own Attitude

Like a rudder that guides the ship along its journey, so do our attitudes guide our lives. Studies show a strong correlation between attitude and success. Think of an athlete preparing for an event or an employee seeking a promotion. Ever hear the phrase, "you need to have a winning attitude"? Attitudes are the guide of our lives.

Negative attitudes can hinder our chances of succeeding. There are many that live by the quote "If you have a negative attitude about a future outcome in your life, it will usually come true." You'll never see a successful athlete, for example, who doubts their abilities, or goes into every game thinking they're going to lose.

Caution: Negative Attitudes are Contagious

Example: While enrolling in next year's math class, you overhear a student who had the same math class and teacher saying all kinds of negative things. You are immediately overwhelmed with dread, and over the next couple of weeks your negative feelings evolve into sheer anxiety.

Bad attitudes like the example described above are almost never your own; like a bad cold, you catch it from someone else. There many reasons why a student may not like a particular class. Maybe they were tardy every day, never did homework, or paid attention to the lessons. You mean to tell me that not one of the students in that class was successful? Why can't you be one of the successful ones?

Be aware of **your own attitude**; and if it is bad, revisit your goals and recommit yourself to them. If you think positive and put on a smile then before you know it, your bad attitude is gone.

Don't be infected by the negative attitudes of others'; instead, keep looking towards your goals in order to stay on track.

Inequalities

Equal to, greater, or less than, too
For any two numbers, it always comes true

Numbers not equal, "a" and "b"
One is greater, as you will see

Less than, greater than, no equal sign
Inequalities arise; it's a matter of time

Operations applied to solving equations
Solve inequalities no matter the occasion

Just one more thing I have to sing
Multiply or divide by a negative thing

Multiplying or dividing by a negative number
Reverses the symbol, in case you wondered

In life, inequalities are woefully sad
Thanks to math poetry, we're a little more glad

Inequalities in Two Variables

Linear inequalities in two variables
Graph of a line is part of the scenario

Just sketch the graph of the given line
If the inequality is strict, it's dashed all the time

The line divides the plane in two regions
Solutions in one of them, we really need to see them

Choose from a region, a point to test
Into the inequality, I'll tell you the rest

If the point works, we shade that side
Otherwise we shade the other with pride

Systems of Linear Inequalities

Linear inequalities simultaneously solved
A region of solutions in the plane has evolved

Just sketch the graphs of the lines in the system
The line is dashed for strict ones, listen

Two or more lines divide the plane
So many regions, I'm going insane

Testing a point from each region
Into the inequalities, I'll tell you the reason

The point that works for the entire system
Is contained in the region where solutions subsist in

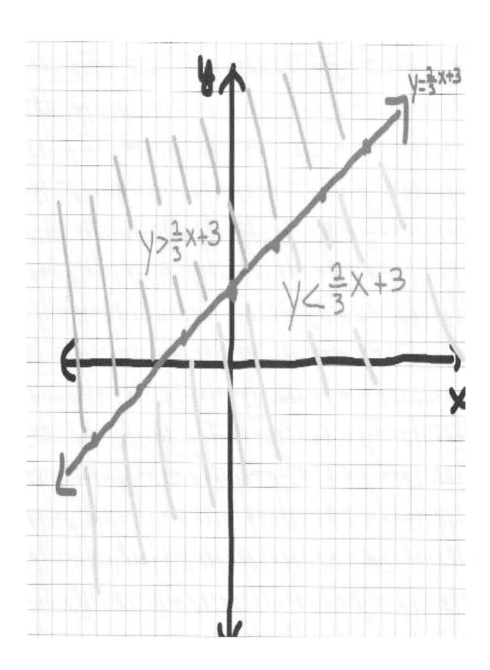

$y = \frac{1}{3}x + 3$

$y > \frac{1}{3}x + 3$

$y < \frac{1}{3}x + 3$

Completing the Square

Roots of quadratics found many ways
Completing the square, we learn today

Put it into standard form
Set to zero, a mathematical norm

When half the linear coefficient squared
Equals the constant term out there

Call it a perfect square trinomial
Yes, it becomes a squared binomial

Squared binomials, we can solve
By square-rooting both sides of the equation involved

But sometimes it happens, please don't stare
Our trinomial is not a perfect square

We must complete it; it's what we do
A balancing act will get us through

Combine to the constant, what needs to be done
A perfect square trinomial will be won

Balance both sides and then you're through
A perfect square trinomial is there for you

Quadratic Formula

A shortcut to completing the square
The quadratic formula will get you there

"a" is the coefficient of the squared term
"b" from the linear one, so I learned

You get a constant, call it "c"
Plug it into the formula, please

Just take negative "b," plus or minus
Square root symbol right behind us

b-squared minus four a-c
Under the radical, you will see

All divided by 2a
Carefully simplify; you'll be okay

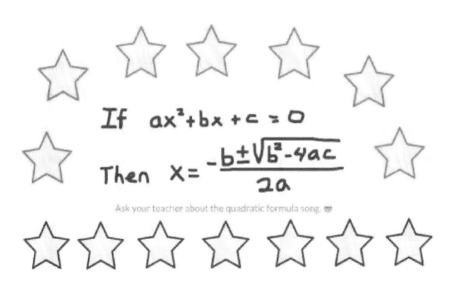

If $ax^2 + bx + c = 0$

Then $x = \dfrac{-b \pm \sqrt{b^2 - 4ac}}{2a}$

Ask your teacher about the quadratic formula song.

Imaginary Numbers

It's hard to imagine an existence without numbers
Take the square of what? I'd have to wonder

Thankfully in our universe, numbers are the key
But we still can't square root negatives of these

So we got creative and began to see
A square root of negative one for thee

They call it i, cause probably
It's an imaginary number, look and see

Just take the square root like you normally do
Place the i, and then you're through

Numbers of the form a + bi
Call them complex, you can imagine why

a - bi a complex conjugate
Sign of the imaginary part is opposite

Imagining square roots in a negative universe
Solutions to equations where normally not traversed

Picture Day

It's that time of the year, let's be clear
We're taking your picture, no need to fear

In the auditorium they're waiting for you
To get in line, and get you through

So remember to put on your very best smile
Your yearbook picture is there for a while

School IDs and community
Your picture helps identify thee

So head on down and get it done
Smile for the camera and have some fun

MEA Break

It's time for a break, you've been working hard
A four-day weekend to play in the yard

Get outside and have some fun
No video games, you need some sun

Don't forget homework and daily review
Helps with grades and learning too

Use your judgement and stay out of trouble
You know what I'm saying: we don't live in a bubble

Sunday night comes really quick
So get your work done, you won't feel sick

Come Monday morning, I'll see you here
To continue our work and finish the year

Operations with Imaginary Numbers

Adding or subtracting imaginary numbers?
It's combining like terms, in case you wondered

Just combine coefficients of imaginary terms
Then combine real parts, no need for concern

Want to multiply complex numbers?
FOIL the binomials at the roll of thunder

Just remember that the square of i
It's negative one, just imagine why

Want to divide complex numbers?
Find the conjugate of the term down under

A clever version of number one
Formed by conjugates, no need to run

Multiply top and bottom by your clever number
It's how we divide, in case you wondered

Discriminant

In life we have inequalities and discrimination
It's dividing our world and hurting our nation

But thanks to math poetry the world is better
We learn about discriminants from the quad formula letters

Real, imaginary or just one solution
A quadratic's discriminant helps the confusion

It's b squared minus 4 a c
The quadratic formula helps you see

If discriminant's a positive, greater than 0
Two real solutions are clearly seen though

If discriminant's a negative, if this is true
Two imaginary solutions come looking for you

If discriminant's a zero, just one solution
Yes that's one, no need for confusion

A square root symbol, a key to understanding
The discriminants work; that is so outstanding

So even though discrimination is wrong
The quadratic's discriminant plays a sweet song

Sketching the Graph

Find solution points, put them in a table
Plot them on a graph, no doubt you are able

Plot the intercepts and check for symmetry
Look for patterns that will help you graphically

You'll sketch the graph like a master
Extra practice makes you faster

X-Y Intercepts

A graphical sketch should include
Any intercepts that it has for you

x-intercept is found by making y zero
If x is zero , the y-intercept is clear, though

So plot your intercepts, no need to worry
Just substitute zero, you'll find them in a hurry

Study Tip 3: Be in the Here and Now

Example: Upon arriving to school, Sarah realized she left the milk out on the kitchen counter, and when she gets home from school, she is bound to get a lecture on kitchen responsibility. When she got to math class, it was all she could think about; she texted her friends for moral support, and mentally rehearsed what she was going to say when she got home. She didn't understand or remember much of what went on in class that day, because she was so preoccupied with her dilemma. It is human nature to occasionally get preoccupied with things over which we have no control. Unfortunately for Sarah, she now has even more to be preoccupied with, like all she missed by not being mentally present during her school day.

To be in the here and now means to mentally focus on the things in front of you; that is, what you can control. During class, there was nothing Sarah could do about the milk left on the counter; thinking about it just caused her more trouble by falling behind in school. Successful students ignore the negative distractions that occur outside the classroom. They put away computers or phones, unless they are being used for class. Be in the "Here and Now!"

Symmetry of Graphs

Symmetry is beautiful and so mathematical
For sketching graphs, it's very practical

If negative y gives the same function back
x-axis symmetry is mixed within the stack

When negative x ends up the same
Symmetry with y goes with the grain

A negative x and negative y
Function unchanged, I began to cry

But no need to cry, it's just unchanged
Origen symmetry, it's one of those thangs

It's good to know our symmetry
To help us graph more easily

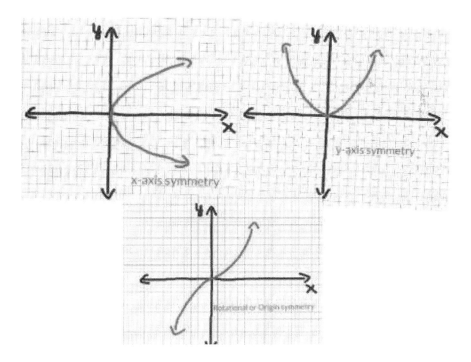

47

Domain and Range

Relation in two variables, inputs and outputs
Usually x in, and y out to us

Set of all inputs, called the Domain
Only these numbers can enter the same

Read the graph, from left to right
Domain is right out there, in plain sight

Undefined values, a mathematical sin
To the domain, they will never go in

From the domain, into the relation
Out comes the range, our next sensation

The set of all outputs, read from the graph
From lowest to highest, so please don't laugh

Domain and range may sound so strange
But they're just mere words like "home on the range."

Functions

Input and output, domain and range
What's your function? sounds pretty strange

For every input, just one out
A function's definition said with a shout

Vertical line test from the graph
Touches one point, a function at last

When the horizontal touches one point, too
A one-to-one function has got to come true

A special relation between two variables
Call it a function, say it in stereo

Even and Odd Functions

When a function's symmetrical about the y
You can call it even, no need to try

And sometimes the function's odd like me
Its graph has origin symmetry

An analytic test for even or odd
Put negative x into the input pod

If the same function comes back to you
An even function is there in cue

But if the function comes back a negative
The function's odd, and sensitive

Combinations of Functions

Multiply or divide, add or subtract
Functions combined as a matter of fact

When adding or subtracting, combine like terms
Down to one function with much less concern

Multiply or divide? Please don't forget
Exponent properties will get you through it

Multiplying terms with like bases
Add the exponents and off to the races

Dividing terms is just the inverse
Subtract the exponents for our next verse

Now the part we talk Domain
Of functions combined it's quite insane

Elements of the domain in common with all
Domain of the combo, please make a call

Relative Max or Min

Lowest within a neighborhood of points
The relative min is first to anoint

From decreasing to increasing across the graph
A relative minimum can be seen at last

When changing from increasing to decreasing
A relative max on the graph is unleashing

Higher than all to its left or right
A relative max wins all the fights

But don't forget it's also true
There's always a max that's greater, too

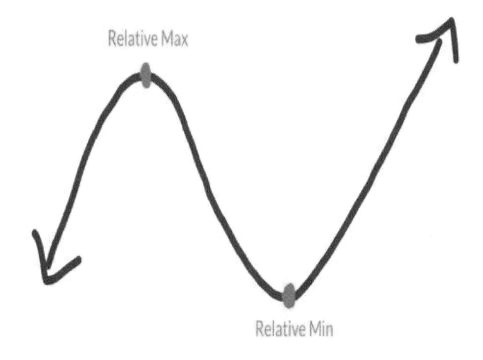

Study Tip 4: Avoiding Distraction

Studies have shown that students who sit in the front two rows of a college classroom have GPAs that average 15% higher than everyone else. Most people at first attribute this to the idea that the more motivated students sit up front. But this is not the case; the reason is that people who sat farther back are subconsciously distracted by the backs of other people's heads. Everything a person sees competes with the learning process. This is enough to make a difference in overall average GPA. What is interesting here is, sometimes, something we're not even aware of can have a measurable difference on our grade outlook.

Even little distractions make a big difference:

- What kind of distractive affect would it be to text friends during a lesson?
- A conversation during a math lesson?
-

Focus on the here and now:

- Do everything you can to focus and avoid distractions.
- Go out of your way to get involved with what's currently going on in class.
- Try to think of questions to ask during the lesson

Thanksgiving

Life has challenges, and can knock you down
Time to be thankful for getting off the ground

So very thankful for this holiday
No more school for the next 4 days

Turkey, pie, mashed potatoes and stuffing
Turkey day football, no I'm not bluffing

Friends and family coming together
Debating issues, and discussing weather

Relax, enjoy and have a blast
Monday's coming, it goes by fast

Don't forget to take some time
Review your school work, if you'd be so inclined

Just a couple of minutes per day
You'll remember better, what can I say?

So Happy Thanksgiving and see you soon
Bright and early, no sleeping till noon

Composite Functions

No cosmetics, or clusters in the cosmos
Or a compost site or anything, who knows?

It's a function in, and a function out
A composite function called throughout

Just make one function the other's input
You get the composite on the side of the output

Look to the composite's input function
You'll find the Domain before the luncheon

The output of the input function, see
Outside function's domain in thee

Finding domains, with functions composed
Composite functions smell sweet as a rose

Inverse Functions

Input to output, a function's word
Caterpillars change to butterflies, I heard

Imagine a butterfly changing back
An inverse function does just that

Output to input, interchanged
Function's domain, the inverse's range

Finding the inverse, follow some steps
Just interchange the y and x

The inverse function is there for you
Solve for y, and simplify through

Sometimes we like to use the graph
To find the inverse, I thought you asked

The inverse is just the graph's reflection
Over y equals x, in case you're checking

Butterflies going back in time
A caterpillar back to the starting line

Roots of a Function

Roots of a function, where f-of-x is zero
Not plants and trees, in order to be clear, though

Just make y zero and solve for old x
Roots of the function are what you have next

Don't forget the other synonymous names
x-intercepts or zeros are exactly the same

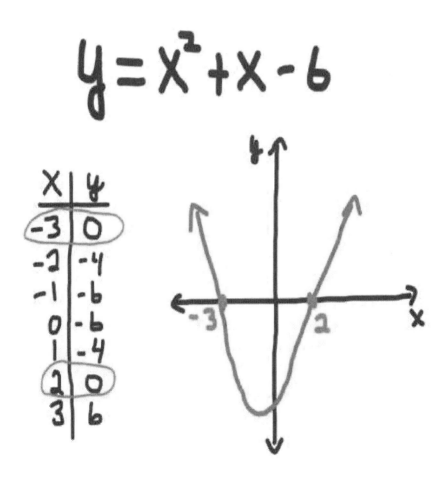

Increasing or Decreasing Functions

Increasing or decreasing, up or down?
A function's graph does not make a sound

Read the graph, from left to right
Decreasing or increasing in perfect sight

Sometimes it doesn't go down or up
A constant interval is surely enough

A function's graph, please know its direction
Derivatives will help, in the next section

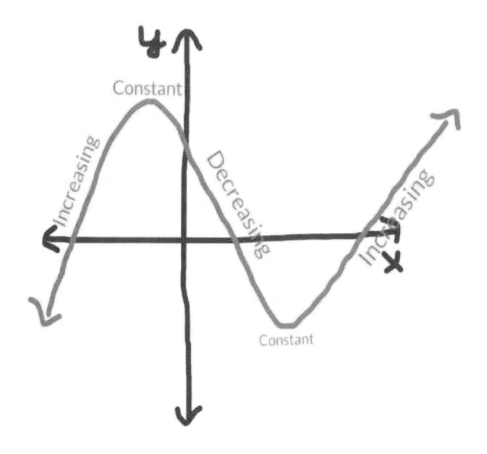

Study Tip 5: Before or After?

Did you know that reviewing notes and homework 3-5 minutes before a math or science class increases comprehension of the new lesson by as much as 60 percent? To get the same benefit in an English or humanities type of class, do your review within 3-5 minutes after class.

Who would've known?

Now, of course, this doesn't mean it is okay to be tardy to English class. The first five minutes of any teacher's instruction is usually the most crucial. It is always best to start out on a ready and positive note, rather than running from behind because you were tardy.

Don't forget the little things that you do will add up and make a big difference. If you master the 29 study tips in this book, all of them combined should have a significant impact on your GPA.

Polynomials

Term whose domain is the set of all reals
Call it a monomial; it's one we can feel

Then there's poly, my favorite bird
Many, many crackers, a prefix word

Put them together to make a polynomial
Many, many terms of beloved monomials

Poly always wants many, many crackers
Between each meal, she's quite the snacker

Adding and Subtracting Polynomials

Combining polynomials through addition and subtraction
Collecting like terms, such complete satisfaction

Exponents and variables of monomials match
Finding like terms is as easy as that

Just combine the terms, the coefficients
Combining polynomials is so efficient

Polynomial Degree

Just add the exponents of the monomial term
You'll find the degree with not much concern

The monomial that contains the highest degree
Is the degree of the polynomial, as you will see

Standard Form Polynomial

Just rewrite the polynomial in descending degree
A standard form polynomial for you and for me

First term in the polynomial, call it the leading
Leading coefficient is out front proceeding

General Expression for a Polynomial Function

$$P(x) = C_0 + C_1 x + C_2 x^2 + C_3 x^3 + \cdots + C_n x^n$$

Example:

$$g(x) = 9 + 3x + 2x^2 - 3x^3 + 6x^7$$

$$\text{or } 6x^7 - 3x^3 + 2x^2 + 3x + 9$$

In a standard form polynomial, the terms are rearranged so that their exponents are in descending order.

To add or subtract polynomial functions, just collect like terms

$$F(x) = 3x^2 - 2x + 7$$
$$g(x) = 5x^2 + 7x - 8$$

$$(F+g)(x) = 3x^2 - 2x + 7 + 5x^2 + 7x - 8$$
$$= 8x^2 + 5x - 1$$

$$(F-g)(x) = 3x^2 - 2x + 7 - (5x^2 + 7x - 8)$$
$$= 3x^2 - 2x + 7 - 5x^2 - 7x + 8$$
$$= -2x^2 - 9x + 15$$

Multiplying Polynomials

Multiply coefficients and add exponents
Multiplying monomials, a main component

Take two polynomials in parentheses
Multiply together and make history

Distribute the monomial from the first polynomial
To the second polynomial, our first testimonial

Next monomial from my first polynomial
Do it again, like the first testimonial

Went through all the terms in the first poly?
You've completely multiplied, it is no folly

Multiplying Binomials

Place the binomials side-by-side
Next we multiply the terms inside

First, outside, inside, last
Call it FOIL and multiply fast

Combine terms from the inside and out
We get the middle, there is no doubt

First times first is first in the trinomial
Multiply the last for the last term, I should know

Binomials multiplied and simplified
Using FOIL and skills applied

Factoring

Now that we've learned multiplying binomials
We invert the process to factor trinomials

Set up your parentheses underneath
No need to fret or grit your teeth

First times first, gives first in the tri
Choose your factors for this to apply

Same for the last, they multiply to the end
You'll find the factors before you count to ten

The outside and the inside give the middle term
Carefully check them, to keep from getting burned

Factoring trinomials into binomials
A part of mathematics you need to get to know

FOIL: First, Inside, Outside, Last

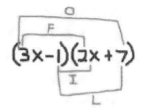
$$6X^2 + 21X - 3X - 7$$
$$6X^2 + 19X - 7$$

General Distribution: Take each term from the first
polynomial, and distribute it to the second. Finish
by collecting like terms and simplifying.

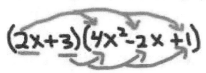
$$8X^3 - 4X^2 + 2X + 12X^2 - 6X + 3$$
$$8X^3 + 8X^2 - 4X + 3$$

Study Tip 6: Try to Work Ahead

Your brain is like a filing cabinet, storing away memories and experiences into different compartments according to its type for easier recall. There is actually a memory technique where if you forget something, you think of everything related to whatever it was you forgot. By doing this, you activate the part of the brain where the memory is stored, possibly triggering recall.

As a student, your brain has to work overtime. Every day it is exposed to different lessons, points of views, homework, social life, discussions, etc. It has to evaluate every bit of new information, determine whether it is important enough to be stored, and then where to store it. Try to imagine a dumpster full of papers thrown in the middle of floor. It's a huge pile of papers, but only a portion is worth keeping; the rest need to be recycled. The important pieces of paper need to be filed away in case they are needed later. This is why it takes the brain 24-72 hours to make sense of new information. Sometimes when teaching a concept that was taught in a previous course, I get comments like, "Why didn't they explain it this way before?" And I'll always tell them, your brain has just had more time to understand. So, how does this knowledge of how the brain stores and metabolizes new information help the student get better grades?

Think of two students, Kong and Sarah:

Using the course syllabus, Kong determines what the lesson will be two days from now. He then reads the lesson and examples from the text, goes online, finds example video lessons on the topic, and then attempts some of the homework. By the day of the lesson, Kong already knows exactly what his questions are going to be. He then follows the lesson intently, even during parts he understood before, always looking for an opportunity to get involved and participate.

Now Sarah, she's about a half a lesson or so behind, it's been a couple of days and now the previous lesson is just beginning to make sense to her.

But this new lesson has her head in a "whirlwind," and she can't even formulate a question.

In the above example, there are no differences between Kong's and Sarah's abilities. But the small difference between being slightly behind in a math class vs. being slightly ahead is going to make a major difference in the grade outcome.

Kong's brain had the advantage in that his brain had been thinking about it long before Sarah's. It's like running a race, giving the other person a 20-minute head start and expecting to win. Personally, out of any study habit I have known, nothing is more effective than working ahead, if you can.

Factoring Trinomials

Factoring trinomials into binomials
Multiplying binomials into trinomials

Inverse of FOIL, undo and recoil
Trinomial factoring of quads stay loyal

List the factors of terms first and last
Try them out, and then have a blast

First times first is the first in the tri
Last times last is the last, don't cry

Outside and the inside give the middle term
You need to check this, a number one concern

Trinomial factoring, learn to do it
Extra practice will help you through it

$$(2x+3)(x-2)$$

$$3x$$

$$-4x$$

$$-x$$

$$2x^2 - x - 6$$

FF   O+I   LL

Trinomial factoring is the inverse of
binomial multiplication. The object is
to find the pair of binomials that
multiply together to give the trinomial

Notice that when we multiply two binomials
into a trinomial, the O and I from FOIL
combine to the middle term of the trinomial.

Ex: $x^2 + 5x + 6$

$$(x+3)(x+2)$$

NHS Poetry Club

It's the NHS society of poet's propriety
Welcome all students; I'd like to say hi to thee

Let's write some poems on subjects like math
Or you make the choice; we'll have a good laugh

No need to worry or be concerned
We're here for fun and to, hopefully, learn

So break out a pen or maybe a pencil
When doing some poetry, it's our best utensil

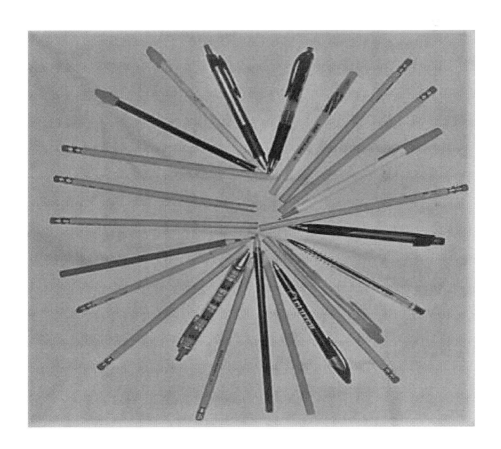

Polynomial Division

A critical point for a timely decision
It's time to learn polynomial division

To place your term, you've got to learn
How to choose with no concern

It's the first term of the old divisor
Into the dividend's first advisor

Just place your term and multiply
Subtract, bring down, we're on the fly

When you've brought down all the terms
A quotients found, you now have learned

If there's anything still remaining
You have a remainder, no need for straining

Quotient plus remainder over divisor
Express the answer, you're all the wiser

$$
\begin{array}{r}
x^2 - 5x - 12 \\
3x+4 \overline{\smash{\big)}\ 3x^3 - 11x^2 - 56x - 48} \\
\underline{3x^3 + 4x^2} \\
-15x^2 - 56x \\
\underline{-15x^2 - 20x} \\
-36x - 48 \\
\underline{-36x - 48} \\
0
\end{array}
$$

Equations of Lines

Slope-Intercept, and Standard Form
Point-Slope equation of lines are the norm

If you know two points, you'll find the slope
Rise over run from a point no joke

Another way to find the slope is next
Think change of y over change of x

Point-Slope line, if you'd be so inclined
You just need a point, and the slope so fine

Take y minus the y-value, and set equal to
Slope times x minus the x-value through

Slope-Intercept form, just solve for y
From point-slope, please give it a try

Slope is the coefficient of the x-term
A constant y-intercept, no need for concern

Easy to graph from its slope and point
Rise over run gets you out of the joint

Parallel lines? Slopes are the same
Opposite reciprocal for perpendicular – insane

Vertical lines are x = k
y = k are horizontal l say

Equations of lines in multiple forms
Do your homework to weather the storm

Rational Functions

Let's be rational, and talk this through
A logical discussion with reason, and clue

If a ratio of integers makes a rational number
Then a ratio of functions sure makes me wonder

A rational function is what this makes
With numerator and denominator to take the cake

A function on top and one down below
A rational function on the hilltop with snow

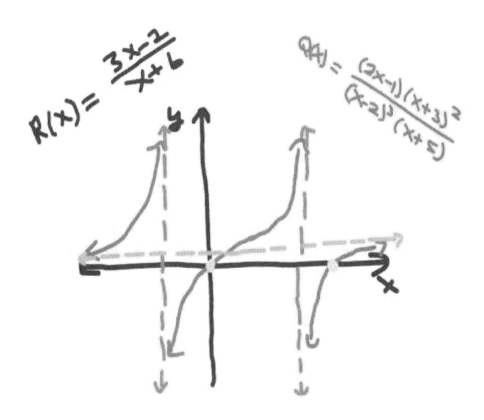

70

Quadratic Function

The degree of this function equals 2
Quadratic functions are nothing new

A special shape, a special name
Path of a ball and parabola the same

An axis of symmetry, a line that cuts through
A parabola's vertex, a min or max, too

Roots are found by a special formula
Called the quadratic I need to inform you of

Quadratics converted to standard form
Complete the square, you've been forewarned

Horizontally and vertically translate the vertex
From the Origin, you know how to work this

Quadratic functions may be second in degree
But nevertheless they're a favorite for me

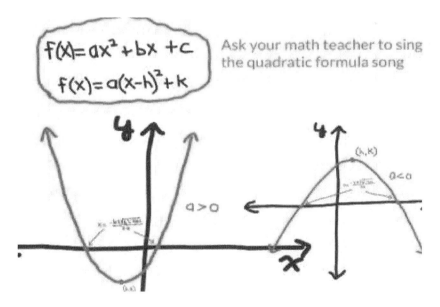

$$f(x) = ax^2 + bx + c$$

$$f(x) = a(x-h)^2 + k$$

Ask your math teacher to sing the quadratic formula song

Review for the Test

Time to review for the test that's coming
So on the day, you won't start running

Linear equations, parallel or perpendicular
Just some things to know in particular

Solving quadratics, completing the square
The quadratic formula is in the air

Find a good friend, who gets good grades
Hang out with them and you'll have it made

When you study together, it's always better
You'll improve your grade, raising the letter

So see you on test day early and bright
Prepared and ready to get this thing right

Study Tip 7: Test Preparation

Doing homework, attending class, Oh the test! Everything comes down to this one moment, a single frame in the movie of my academic life. Class discussions, participation, or a single performance will judge the situation, teachers remind us every day; the most important event on the calendar they say.

It seems unfair that all the hard work in a particular class can be evaluated by just a few simple tests and quizzes, especially if you are like many students who claim they are just no good at taking tests. But we also need to face the facts that testing is not going away soon. Yes, alternative means of assessing students have been explored for decades now, and with all that, we just can't get away from testing. Nobody is going to get through college without having to take a test at some point.

So what about the students who are poor at testing?
If a student has been identified as having a test anxiety issue, and there is an accommodation plan in place, then the teacher follows the plan. But studies have shown that the overwhelming majority of bad test takers have anxiety only because they are not prepared to take the test. Yes, lack of preparation is the major cause of test anxiety. Test preparation is something all students should learn to do. There are online books about how to get good grades, and they usually have a section about test preparation.

Test Preparation Tips

- Prepare as if the test or quiz was a day before the scheduled date. If the test is next Thursday, pretend it is really scheduled for Wednesday.
- Test preparation is not simply done the night before; it is an ongoing process that is done daily.
- Listen to your teacher for hints and clues as to what may be on the test, then take notes.
- Create a compressive list of anything that could be testable. For example, finding the roots using the quadratic formula is something testable.
- Keep up on your daily and weekly reviews. Then re-review everything from the comprehensive test list.
- Make sure you know how to do everything on the list.
- Review any extra notes from instructor, homework or any miscellaneous items.
- Have good diet, exercise and sleep habits.

During Test

- Show up early for class on the day of the test.
- Have all tools, calculators, paper, and extra pencils ready to go before class starts.
- Read all instruction and questions carefully.
- Do all of the easier problems first, skipping anything that you think may cause some trouble. After the easier ones are done, then go back to them.
- Always review your work before handing in.

Winter Break

We've worked really hard and it's time for a break
It's holidays and parties, for goodness sake

Going on vacation until next year
The air is filled with laughter and cheer

No more homework, and no more teachers
No life lessons from thirteen preachers

A time for activities and playing outside
Toboggans, ice castles or taking sleigh rides

Family get-togethers and holiday feasts
Smells from the kitchen, so lovely and sweet

Bringing in the New Year with family and friends
Next year is coming and vacation will end

Make a resolution and stick to it tight
Give it your all, you may have to fight

Set up a goal to do your best
In everything you do and to all the rest

When we get back to start the New Year
We'll start it out right and have a great cheer

Probability

70 percent chance of snow in the morning
Thank you probability, I'll heed the warning

Always there to measure our chances
For winning prizes or going to dances

It's the total number of desired events
Divided by the possible, it's just common sense

Sometimes we try experimentally
To estimate our probability

So whether in practice or just in theory
Knowing probability will help us see clearly

What are the chances?

Counting Principles

How many possible computer passwords?
What's the chance that I'll even be heard?

A fundamental concern in probability
Is to count the possibilities so accurately

Counting numbers or elements in a set
There are different ways to do this yet

Mutually exclusive events happen separately
Not at the same time, you'll see conceptually

Non-mutually exclusive, you have to take care
To not double-count the elements there

Events Independent are unrelated
To what happened before, it's clearly stated

Now the number of ways each event occurs
Multiplied together, that's what I heard

Gives the ways they can happen together
A principle in counting thrown in for measure

Permutations

An ordered arrangement of a set of objects
Permutations for counting, you cannot stop it

It's n factorial, over n minus r factorial
The number of arrangements appears in stereo

How many ways to choose the winner of the race?
Or to select a president or secretary, just in case?

Use permutations for ordered arrangements
You'll count the ways at your next engagement

Combinations

Pepperoni-sausage or sausage-pepperoni
Same kind of pizza says my great Uncle Tony

Combinations of items where order doesn't matter
Counted the same, I couldn't be gladder

Just take the permutations and divide out the repetitions
Arrangements of the same objects are one in cognition

Use the permutation formula and divide by r factorial
You'll find the combinations for various scenarios

Remember the context when deciding what to use
Permutations and combination are counting on you

Study Tip 8: Daily Review

Studies show that within 24 hours, students forget 75 to 80 percent of everything learned in class that day.

However, if the student does a 10 to 15 minute daily review, retention goes up to over 80 percent. A daily review could be immediately attempting math homework, then trying it again later or when you get home, or glancing over examples, old homework or notes. For some subjects, it's a great idea to find other classmates to have a quick 10 to 20 minute reflection about class.

One thing to be cautious about, especially for the weekend, is getting certain homework like math done too quickly, then doing nothing for several days later. For example, during Friday's math class you found the lesson easy, and completed all work within 15 minutes, then did nothing until the following Monday. If you do this, by Monday you will have lost most of your gains in the subject.

It's not enough to say "I have no homework for a particular class, so I can take the day off in that particular subject"; a daily review for all classes should be a daily ritual. Students who get good grades study even when they don't have homework.

Properties of Probability

What are the chances it will happen again?
Does it depend on what already happened then?

Dependent events affect each other
Probability changes into another

Independent events, it does not matter
What happened before won't affect the latter

To find probabilities of sequential events
Multiply their probabilities, it just makes sense

To find probabilities of events A or B
Add the probabilities on the count of three

Union is "or" and intersection is "and"
Let's go to the beach and run through the sand

Either it will happen or it will not
Complementary events sure are hot

So 1 minus the probability of the event occurring
Is the probability that no event is stirring

$$P(A|B) = \frac{P(A \cap B)}{P(B)}$$

The probability of the event A, given the event B has already happened.

$$P(A \cap B) = P(B) \cdot P(A|B)$$

The probability of events A and B happening together when the events are dependent.

$$P(A \cap B) = P(A) \cdot P(B)$$

The probability of events A and B happening together when the events are independent.

$$P(A \cup B) = P(A) + P(B) - P(A \cap B)$$

The probability of the inclusive events A or B

$$P(A \cup B) = P(A) + P(B)$$

The probability of the mutually exclusive events A or B.

Random Variables in Probability

Two out of three, or three out of five
A random variable in this case applies

Repeated events of the same type
How many successes will clear up the hype?

Probability of success to the power of how many
Times the probability of failure to a power, if any

Next we multiply by n-C-r
r out of n chances you'll win a new car

Our random variable will count your successes
Out of how many, you need to address this

Expected Value

What kind of outcome would you expect?
Will you win any money if you placed a bet?

Mathematical expectation in probability
Will answer these questions most certainly

Take the probability of winning the prize
Times its value, a word from the wise

What you get is an average return
If pay any more I would be very concerned

A weighted average of expected payouts
Mathematical expectation will take you way out

Happy New Year

Back from the holidays, it's 2018
A New Year started, can't wait to be seen

It's back to the grind with books and iPads
Two weeks till the end of the quarter, I'm so glad

Friends and staff are here to greet
We say Happy New Year when we first meet

So Happy New Year to each and everyone
I hope this new year will bring you much fun

Compound Events

An event composed of several outcomes
Not so simple, like taxable income

Compound events will happen together
Like snow and rain at the same time in weather

Mutually exclusive, not at the same time
It's one or the other, we must draw the line

Inclusive events, both happen at once
At the same time, like days in a month

Keywords "and" or "then" or "both"
Multiply probabilities, and take good notes

Called an intersection of events we mention
Happening together without a question

A union of events, keyword "or"
Just add the probabilities and run for the door

With inclusive events , subtract the intersection
We never count twice, as learned in this section

Multiplying-Dividing Rational Functions

Factor the numerators, factor the denominators
Cancel the common to simplify them out of here

Multiply across as you do with fractions
Using techniques from the polynomial faction

Invert and multiply when you divide
Don't forget to simplify and take it in stride

Multiplying and dividing rational functions
A fundamental skill in the algebraic junction

$$\frac{10x-40}{x^2-6x+8} \cdot \frac{x+3}{5x+15}$$

$$\frac{\overset{2}{10}(x-4)}{(x-4)(x-2)} \cdot \frac{x+3 \,\, \overset{1}{}}{5(x+3)}$$

$$\frac{2}{x-2}$$

Radical Expressions

Radical expressions, faces contorted
While teaching the lesson, my students aborted

Now's a good time for some math poetry
For fractional exponents to help us clearly

Take one over the index of the radicand
A fractional power will make the stand

Radical x or radical y
Just fractional powers, I'm telling no lies

Study Tip 9: Weekly Reviews

If you want to bring your retention to at least 90 percent, you must do a weekly review for every class. In just 10 to 15 minutes, you can review all the notes, homework, papers, reports, books or chapters read and more. The effects of the daily and weekly review cannot be underestimated. For the extra time it takes one day per week, the payout in retention and understanding is huge.

The benefit of the weekly review is so great that the time spent in doing it is sometimes subtracted by how much less time you'll need in a week because you did it. It's interesting, because those who plan their study time on an as-needed basis usually end up putting in more overall study time, and with less benefit, than those who conduct daily, weekly, and monthly reviews on a continual basis.

Just remember to follow your periodic review schedule, and you will be surprised by the progress you make towards your goals.

Extra tip: Most courses have a cutoff of at least 90 % in order to earn an A, but conducting a weekly review only brings retention to an average of 90 %. So, what if you are trying to earn an A, and you don't want to cut it so close? What some people do is review beyond what is required for the class. This could be pursuing a topic deeper, or doing extra homework from the text, going on the internet, or even learning more of what is required.

For example: If you just go an extra 10% beyond what is required, your average retention is now 90% of 110%, which is like an overall 99%. Get the idea?

Graph of the Square Root Function

Mr. H, your teacher, they call a square
Is this because he has no hair?

We have a function that's called this, too
It has no hair, just roots for you

It has a domain called positive real
Same for the range that cooks our meals

Our square root's graph, translates vertically
By adding or subtracting, don't take this personally

Horizontal translation, yes, left or right
From inside the function an opposite flight

Our square roots graph, its shape retained
With respect to translations, it stays the same

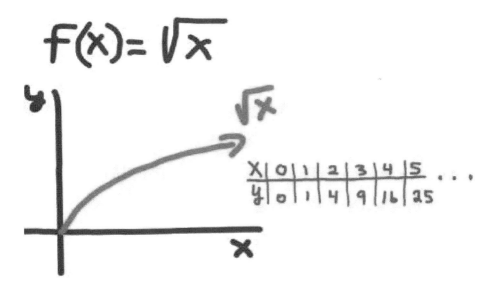

Radical Equations

Equations with variables underneath the radical
You need to solve these, no need to get fanatical

Yes, a radical equation is what it is
One must learn this by the next quiz

Just isolate the radical to equations one side
Then raise to the power of the index inside

Next we solve using algebraic techniques
Your friends will envy, and call you a geek

Don't forget to check the solution
To the original equation to avoid confusion

Solution doesn't work, we call extraneous
Your friends will bow down and call you the brainiest

$$\sqrt[w]{x}^{\wedge} = X$$

$$\sqrt{x-2} = 9$$
$$\sqrt{x-2}^2 = 9^2$$
$$x-2 = 81$$
$$x = 83$$

$$\sqrt[3]{x+1} = 4$$
$$\sqrt[3]{x+1}^3 = 4^3$$
$$x+1 = 64$$
$$x = 63$$

$$\sqrt[5]{x} = 2$$
$$\sqrt[5]{x}^5 = 2^5$$
$$x = 32$$

Study Tip 10: Quarterly Reviews

By now everyone has heard that cramming for final exams is not a good study practice. But this is only true for those who rely on the cram as their sole means for review. To the student who has mastered the daily, weekly, and monthly review system, preparing for a final is just another review day of perhaps, 15-20 minutes. It is only recommended that several sessions take place when studying for a major assessment.

Example: When studying for a math test, look at old homework and quizzes, read through examples and rework some of the earlier homework. Key in on any topics your instructor may have emphasized during previous instruction. Also, don't forget to prepare as if the test is one day prior to when it actual happens. Revisit Study Tip 7 for a more comprehensive list.

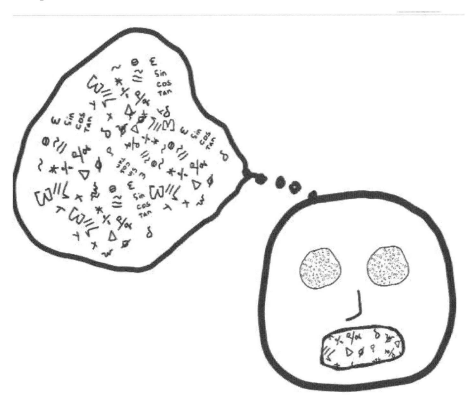

Rational Roots Theorem

Polynomial degree with roots of same number
Some may be rational, you just have to wonder

A rational roots theorem will help you find
The rational roots of any kind

Just make a list of constant term factors
Write them on down like a seasoned redactor

The leading coefficient has factors, too
Write these down also, we're not yet through

Polynomial roots come from these ratios
Constant to Leading, factors in place though

Now substitute your ratios into the poly
If it gives you zero, a root with no folly

From the root, a factor is found
Now polynomial division will get you off the ground

Division will give you the other factors
The rational roots theorem makes you a transactor

Horizontal Asymptotes

Asymptotic behavior of the horizontal type
A behavior of the graph on the ends with no gripe

Closer and closer, a graphical approach
A particular value at the edge of the coast

An imaginary line at infinity plus or minus
Horizontal asymptotes of the graph are right behind us

Comparing the numerator and denominator degrees
Horizontal asymptotes are really a breeze

Degree of numerator less than denominator
y equals zero is a horizontal commentator

Numerator and denominators degrees are equal
Ratio of coefficients will lead the sequel

When the numerators degree is greater, too
No horizontal asymptotes are there for you

Asymptotic behaviors of people are sad
But for graphical patterns, it's all we had

Vertical Asymptotes

Undefined values never enter the domain
No points on the graph are there to remain

A point where the denominator is equal to zero
Called vertical Asymptotes or holes to be clear, though

Even or odd, a vertical asymptotes degree
Just like roots of a function, as you'll see

The graph it approaches up or down
Positive or negative infinity bound

When the approach from both sides is down-up or up-down
It's an odd vertical asymptote like Krusty the Clown

When the approach is the same, down-down or up-up
An even vertical asymptote, I tell you "what's up?"

$x = k$, an equation form
Vertical asymptotes from the denominator are born

Even and Odd Roots

Input the value of x in the function
If the output is zero, it's a root in conjunction

x-intercepts or zeros they're called
Or roots of the function are the same for all

The graph either goes through or touches the x-axis
Roots of the function or a zero for our taxes

If the root is even, it does not go through
You can tell by the exponent, it's even for you

When a root is odd according to the exponent
Graph goes through the x-axis that moment

Roots, zeros, x-intercepts or whatever
Synonymous terms that will make you sound clever

Rapid Curve Sketch

A rational function, we graph in conjunction
Putting it together without a malfunction

Roots, y-intercepts, horizontal and vertical
Determining asymptotes a part that is critical

Even or odd vertical asymptotes or roots
Determines the graphical pattern to boot

Very systematic, a graph so dramatic
A rapid curve sketch is part of mathematics

Study Tip 11: Scheduling Breaks

You're studying for an important test or you have an extra-long reading assignment that you just want to get done. It is tempting at this point to want to plunge through without a break to save time. But are you really saving time? Studies show that the brain can only rock steady for 50-minute intervals, followed by mindless 10-minute breaks. Therefore, anything beyond 50 minutes without a break is wasted effort. Two 50-minute study sessions with appropriate breaks are actually more effective than 6 to 8 hours straight with few to no breaks at all.

Transforming Functions

The graph of the parent from which it started
A transformed function has now departed

Was stretched horizontally and vertically in life
A transformed function has defeated the strife

Navigating through hurdles horizontally and vertically
A transformed function translates perfectly

Coming to the end, a destination reached
A transformed function will come to a screech

Reflecting back from whence it came
Functions transformed are never the same

Oh transformed function forever renewed
A brand new form and beautiful, too

$f(x) + k$ — Vertical Shift up by k.

$f(x) - k$ — Vertical Shift down by k.

$f(x + h)$ — Horizontal Shift to the left by h.

$f(x - h)$ — Horizontal Shift to the right by h.

$af(x)$ — Vertical Dilation with factor of a.

$f(ax)$ — Horizontal Dilation with factor 1/a.

Vertical and Horizontal Stretch or Shrink

Sometimes we stretch and then we shrink
Horizontally or vertically before we blink

Function's output, by a constant, multiplied
A shrink or stretch so vertically applied

Input multiplied, by a constant bit
A horizontal dilation by the reciprocal of it

A horizontal of vertical stretch or shrink
What type of dilation is making me think?

Vertical and Horizontal Shift

To translate a graph vertically up or down
Add/Subtract a constant all the way around

If you add a constant to the input variable
The function shifts left, an opposite scenario

To shift your graph onto the right
Subtract from the input, then put it in flight

Exponential Functions

Certain functions are mathematically essential
Especially functions that are called exponential

Input variable, the function's exponent
An exponential function's main component

y equals "a" times "b" to the "x"
The standard equation read the text

When b is a number greater than 1
It's growing exponentially and we're having fun

When b is between 1 and 0
Decaying exponentially with nothing to fear, though

When solving exponentials, we use our logs
That's the next lesson, to clear the fog

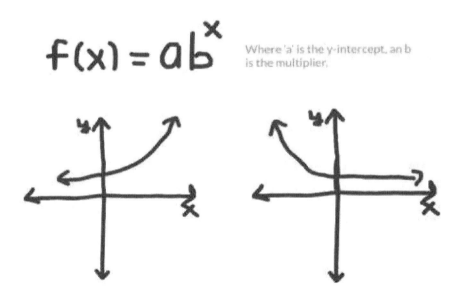

$$f(x) = ab^x$$

Where 'a' is the y-intercept, an b is the multiplier.

Study Tip 12: Never Tune Out

Bobby realizes that Mr. H's lesson was about a topic he learned last year. So he tunes out and either uses the opportunity to get caught up on other stuff, or to just take a mental vacation by playing games on his phone. Much to Bobby's disappointment, he fails the next test. He swears up and down that he knew the stuff, and was surprised at how little he remembered.

Situations like Bobby's are common. When in college, taking calculus for the first time really worried me. Many students in the course had already taken calculus in high school. It seemed I would be at a disadvantage, but what surprised me was that it appeared that those who had the course before did worse than those who hadn't.

One possible reason for this is that our brains are primed to recall big picture ideas, overall topics, and lessons learned. But it finds details less important. Sort of like remembering that you had lunch two days ago, but don't remember what you had. The only problem is the test will be on what we had for lunch.

When in a class, just remember to always pay attention as if it was the first time ever hearing the topic or question. Otherwise, you too will forget the details of what is needed on the test. Remember, the more exposures to a topic, the closer it gets to long-term memory. This is why you pay attention, even if you think you don't need to.

Definition of a Log

b to the x equals c
Log base b of x is thee

b the base, raised to a power
Equals the argument of the log this hour

Think of your logs as just another way
To write exponentials any time of day

Logarithmic Functions

Exponential functions are one to one
They have an inverse, please tell everyone

A logarithmic function is what it's called
Inverted exponential says it all

It has a base, they call it b
Same as the exponential as I can see

Take it to the power of what the log equals
You get the argument of the log's next sequel

An exponential function, the log's inverse
Logarithmic functions rule the universe

Properties of Logs

Properties of logs, we have a few
So I wrote a poem to help you through

Log of a product is the sum of logs
A useful rule for lifting the fog

Sometimes with logs we take the difference
A log of a quotient would be my inference

Then, of course, the log of a power
Multiple of logs, it turns this hour

Base of the log and exponent the same
Cancel them out, not playing any games

Properties of logs will help you through
Read the blog, I know it's true

Exponential Equations

Solved an equation that's exponential
Using logs, it's nothing special

Just isolate base and exponent to one side
Now take the log and let it ride

Log of a power, a multiple of a log
Equation solved, you're out of the fog

A pattern that helps, a shortcut for you
I'll tell you next and then we're through

If b to the x is equal to c
Then x equals log c over log b

Logarithmic Equations

Logarithmic equations need to be solved
From inside the argument, so get involved

Use the properties of logs to combine
To a log of a single argument refined

Next, convert to exponential form
Solve for the argument, a solution is born

Don't forget to check your solutions
Extraneous ones, no need for confusion

If they violate the log's input domain
Discard those ones, keep those that remain

Exponential functions with logs so essential
Logarithmic equations are quite monumental

Logistic Functions

Growing exponentially, but not forever
Logistics models for populations wherever

Grows first fast, then approaches a limit
Leveling out as populations aren't infinite

Populations like C divided and wary
By 1 plus ab to the negative x, scary

Logistics functions for limited growth
Humankind so finite, yet infinite to boast

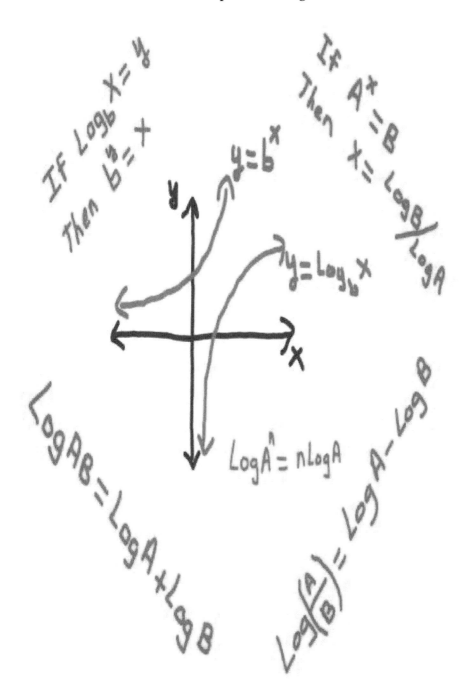

If $Log_b X = Y$
Then $b^y = X$

If $A^x = B$
Then $X = LogB/LogA$

$y = b^x$

$y = Log_b X$

$Log A^n = n Log A$

$Log AB = Log A + Log B$

$Log(\frac{A}{B}) = Log A - Log B$

Study Tip 13: No Such Thing as Luck

Never rely on dishonest measures such as cheating. Studies show that people who rely on cheating are statistically almost 2 GPA points lower than those who rely on their own honest efforts. For example, while taking a state math exam where 60 percent of the participants get a particular question wrong; what are your chances of copying the correct answer from the person next to you? Your best chances are always better when you know the answers yourself. Just follow the other study tips throughout this book, and you will have no trouble preparing honestly, with no luck.

Quadratic Form

An exponential equation just for thee
It looks quadratic from what I see

Performed a substitution, it even got better
It's now quadratic right down to the letter

Solved the quad as I normally do
Then back substituted, and carried on through

Exponential equations in quadratic form
Solved by substituting, you've been forewarned

Identifying Functions from Graphs

Identifying functions through graphical patterns
Their special shapes will turn on the lantern

A linear function runs a straight line
Constant rate of change is there all the time

Quadratic function, a path of a ball
Opens up or downward accepting the call

For power models, a positive domain
A single monomial term is insane

Our exponentials are quite essential
Growth or decay is truly monumental

Knowing functions through patterns in graphs
A part of mathematics I know we can grasp

Identifying Functions from Tables

Linear, quadratic, exponential, or power
We learn to identify through tables this hour

An Add-Add pattern, a constant theme
The function's linear, I heard in a dream

An Add-Multiply pattern increases exponentially
Exponential functions will grow monumentally

A function with power, the star of the hour
A Multiply-Multiply rule of brain power

Last but not least, a quadratic function
Let's talk this out at our next luncheon

Subtract consecutive y's from the table
A first set of differences you truly are able

From the first differences subtract again
A second set of differences we look to them

If the second differences are constantly the same
Your function's quadratic, a powerful name

Study Tip 14: Don't Wait!

Michael didn't understand Monday's lesson on multiplying binomials. He said, "I'll come after school Friday and get some extra help." On Tuesday the factoring lesson was taught. Since factoring is the inverse of multiplying, he probably had trouble understanding factoring. He probably had trouble with Wednesday's solve quadratics by factoring lesson also, and by the time Thursday's lesson comes along, Michael may be totally lost in the class.

Now, because one lesson is connected to the one before, Michael will probably need help for everything covered during the week. Even worse, depending on the level of the high school or college course, Michael could get to a point where he is hopelessly behind, a true but unfortunate fact, and it could happen to any of us if we let down our guard.

Now, if the problem was fixed Monday, at the onset of the trouble, Michael may have never fallen behind to begin with. By getting Monday's lesson down while it is still Monday means that he'll have an easier time with Tuesday's lesson. On any of the given days of the week Michael needs help, he should try to get the help on that day. It's not always possible, but every effort should be made. If you can't make it after school, try to connect with a friend, or just go online and search for what it is you need help with. With the resources available at our fingertips, there is rarely a reason to ever fall behind.

Right Triangle Trig

Opposite, adjacent, and hypotenuse
Relative to the angle of the triangle we use

Trig of right triangles, first thing we learn
When doing trig it's the number one concern

SOH-CAH-TOA, a mnemonic device
Makes memorizing trig exceptionally nice

Sine of the angle, heard the news?
It's opposite over the hypotenuse

Cosine is fine, it's looks like sine
It's the adjacent over the hypotenuse line

Tangent is best; we're off on one next
Opposite over adjacent, its quest

For finding angles or right triangle sides
Right triangle trig is the sure way to ride

$$\text{SOH-CAH-TOA}$$

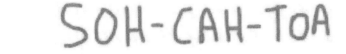

$$\sin \theta = \frac{opp}{hyp} \qquad \cos \theta = \frac{Adj}{hyp} \qquad \tan \theta = \frac{opp}{Adj}$$

$$\sin A = \frac{a}{c} \qquad \sin B = \frac{b}{c}$$
$$\cos A = \frac{b}{c} \qquad \cos B = \frac{a}{c}$$
$$\tan A = \frac{a}{b} \qquad \tan B = \frac{b}{a}$$

The Six Trig Ratios

Sine, Cosine and Tangent please
With SOH-CAH-TOA we memorized these

But three more ratios that can't be missed
Add Cosecant, Secant, Cotangent to the list

Cosecant, the reciprocal of the Sine
Hypotenuse over opposite, all the time

Then there's Secant, hypotenuse over adjacent
Cosine's reciprocal, no need for replacement

One left over, adjacent over opposite
Call it Cotangent to stay on top of it

Reciprocal trig ratios, we have a few
Added to the others makes six for you

Reciprocal Trig Ratios

$$\sin\theta = \frac{1}{\csc\theta} \qquad \cos\theta = \frac{1}{\sec\theta} \qquad \tan\theta = \frac{1}{\cot\theta}$$

$$\sin\theta = \frac{O}{H} \qquad \csc\theta = \frac{H}{O}$$

$$\cos\theta = \frac{A}{H} \qquad \sec\theta = \frac{H}{A}$$

$$\tan\theta = \frac{O}{A} \qquad \cot\theta = \frac{A}{O}$$

Special Right Triangles

A very special day, a very special cause
Special right triangles make me want to pause

Thirty-sixty-ninety, a very special case
Its short leg's half the hypotenuse in place

Multiply the short one by the square root of 3
You'll get the long leg, especially, you'll see

Another special story, another special kind
Forty-five- forty-five isosceles are prime

Legs congruent, so especially true
We'll find the hypotenuse before we get through

To find the hypotenuse, this is what you do
Just multiply the leg by the square root of two

Special Right

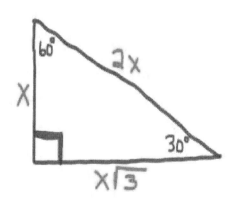
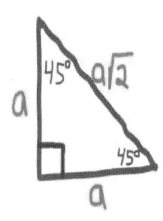

Law of Sines

Our universe is governed by rules and laws
They will be followed, it's in the clause

A certain law in trig you'll find
All triangles must follow the Law of Sines

Ratio of a side to the sine of the opposite angle
Is always the same on any particular triangle

The reciprocal of this law is also applied
The sine of the angle to its opposite side

So if you know an angle and opposite side, too
The Law of Sines will help get you through

$$\frac{\sin B}{12} = \frac{\sin 42}{22}$$

$$\sin B = \frac{12 \sin 42}{22} \approx .3650$$

$$\angle B = \sin^{-1}(.3650) \approx 21.4°$$

$$\angle C = 180 - 42 - 21.4 \approx 116.6°$$

$$\frac{C}{\sin 116.6} = \frac{22}{\sin 42}$$

$$C = \frac{22 \sin 116.6}{\sin 42} \approx 29.4 \text{ in}$$

111

Law of Cosines

Just when we thought we knew the law
The Law of Cosines is what we saw

Squared c equals squared "a" plus squared b
Minus 2 times a-b cosine C

Just the Pythagorean Theorem in disguise
Cosine of 90 is zero to the wise

When we know a triangle's three sides
Cosines' formula for angles applies

CosA equals squared b plus squared c
Minus the square of 'a' let's see

Take all this over 2bc
Cosine inverse gets the angle for thee

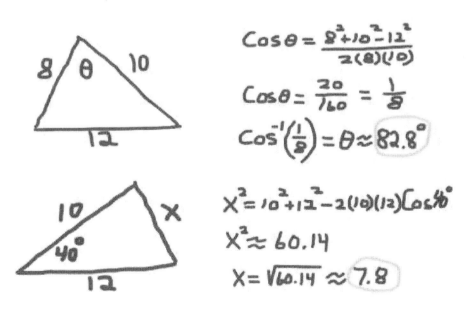

$$Cos\theta = \frac{8^2 + 10^2 - 12^2}{2(8)(10)}$$

$$Cos\theta = \frac{20}{160} = \frac{1}{8}$$

$$Cos^{-1}\left(\frac{1}{8}\right) = \theta \approx 82.8°$$

$$X^2 = 10^2 + 12^2 - 2(10)(12)Cos40°$$

$$X^2 \approx 60.14$$

$$X = \sqrt{60.14} \approx 7.8$$

Study Tip 15: Manage Your Time Wisely

In the middle of math class, the teacher is going over a lesson Joeann has heard before. What a great time, she thinks, to get some reading done on Civil War history. Or maybe she thinks she can take a mental break, catch up on a text, or play a game. After all, the stuff the teacher is talking about is stuff she already knows. Two weeks later, Joeann is scratching her head, wondering what went wrong on the math test. She thought she knew everything that was taught over the last couple weeks. In fact, it was one of the easier units of the year. See Study Tip 12 for answer.

The fact that someone would tune out in the middle of a class, because it's stuff they already know, violates many of the study tips throughout this book. Any moment where the class is doing something that you are already comfortable with, is an opportunity for you to immerse yourself and participate to your fullest. This will lead to better outcomes in the long run.

If you are properly managing your schedule, you will have a set time for doing set things. There should almost never be a time where you work on another subject area during the time of another subject. Math during math, English during English; it's as simple as that. Stick to your plan, and don't forget to schedule breaks.

Area of a Triangle

Half the base times the height of a triangle
A triangle's area is given on the go

Thanks to the Law of Sines tonight
There's another way to get the height

The sine of the angle times either side adjacent
Gives the function height of the triangles placement

The base is the other adjacent side
Not used for the height it does abide

Put this together on the count of three
An area formula is coming to thee

Just half the product of any two sides
Times the sine of the angle between coincides

Heron's Formula

A bird of fresh water, grey or blue,
This great bird catches fish for you

So a triangle area, or a long-legged bird
Heron's formula for triangles are heard

Take half the perimeter, yes divide by 2
Call it semiperimeter; it's what we do

Take semiperimeter minus each of the sides
Multiply together with semiperimeter inside

Put it together underneath the square root
We get the area of the triangle to boot

Trigonometric Models

Sine, Cosine, and don't forget tangent
They all tied for first, at the math beauty pageant

The sinusoids, yes sine and cosine
They model behavior of a circular kind

Periodic in nature of 360 degrees
Seasons and weather, they model the breeze

Wagon wheels, and Ferris Wheels, the tide coming in
The deal is sealed and our sinusoids win

Sine and cosine, such active models
Of real life scenarios, not genies in bottles

Circle

Set of all points, equidistant from the center
Describes a circle, to my thoughts it entered

An analytic equation is there for you
It gives the center and the radius, so true

Derived from the formula, used for distance
Distance from center, is constant this instant

Radius squared, or square of the distance
Center h,k this very instance

Plot the center, use the radius
Around the circle our thoughts are craziest

In art and history, things come around
A circular fashion, mathematically sound

Study Tip 16: Listen to Other People's Questions

Jerome asked a question about a math problem that Jill already had worked out. So while the instructor went over the problem with the class, Jill thought it would be a good time to catch up with a text from a friend. Unfortunately, Jill got an almost identical question wrong on the test two weeks later. What happened?

Students think that if it wasn't a question they thought of, or pertaining to a problem they had trouble with, they are excused from interacting with the question and response. The problem, especially in math, is there could be ways of thinking that you may not have thought of before, maybe another method. Plus, if you are to get the concept into your long-term memory, you need as many interactions with the concept as you can get. All questions from all students should be treated as an opportunity to engage with the topic and deepen your understanding.

Always Stay Tuned In

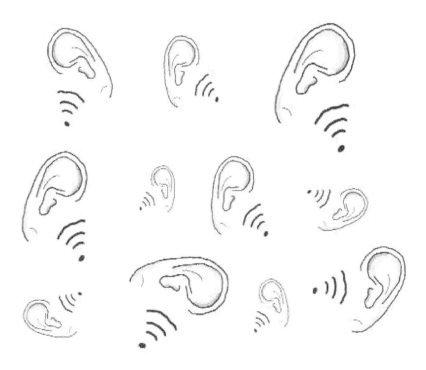

Angle of Rotation

Start with a ray and rotate around
An angle is generated without any sound

The initial side, where rotation begins
The terminal side is where rotation ends

When rotating the ray in the direction counterclockwise
A positive angle appears like the sunrise

So counterintuitive for angles negative
We rotate clockwise, it's just so repetitive

An angle of rotation, initial to terminal
When doing trig, it's nothing personal

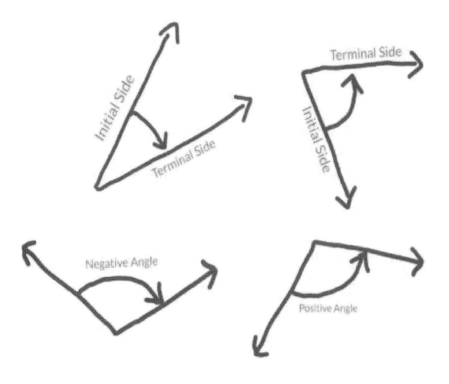

Standard Position Angles

The positive x-axis, the initial side
Angle of rotation, standard position applied

From the positive x, we rotate the ray
Its standard position, we can do this all day

It terminates in quadrants 1 to 4
A reference angle gets you so much more

Acute angle formed with the terminal side and x
Reference angles for trig are simply the best

Coterminal angles are also formed
Same terminal side, many angles conform

Reference angle and terminal side
A reference triangle is made to abide

Legs are positive or negative by direction
Hypotenuse positive it's part of the lesson

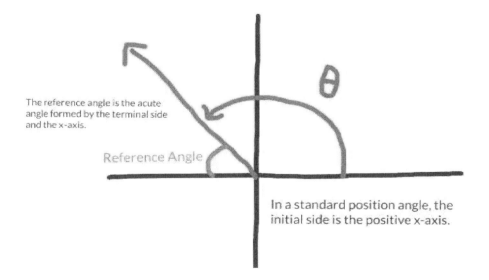

The reference angle is the acute angle formed by the terminal side and the x-axis.

Reference Angle

θ

In a standard position angle, the initial side is the positive x-axis.

Point on a Terminal Side

A Point on the angle's terminal side
From standard position our trig ratios fly

A reference triangle drawn from the point
To find trig ratios, that is the point

Positive or negative, the triangle's legs
The x-y values will give it away

Hypotenuse positive, it's always true
A bit of advice from Pythagoras, too

Our reference triangle's now in place
We'll give the trig ratios with no need to race

Trig of Any Angle

Angle greater than 90 degrees
From standard position, it's one of these

Just make a reference triangle
Then do some trig, it is the way to go

All Students Take Calculus, a catchy phrase
Trig ratios positive or negative won't faze

Don't forget the legs of the tri
Are positive or negative, the direction is why

The hypotenuse always stays positive
Like math poetry, we hear a lot of it

The point (-5,12) lies on the terminal side of an angle, find the value of the six trig ratios.

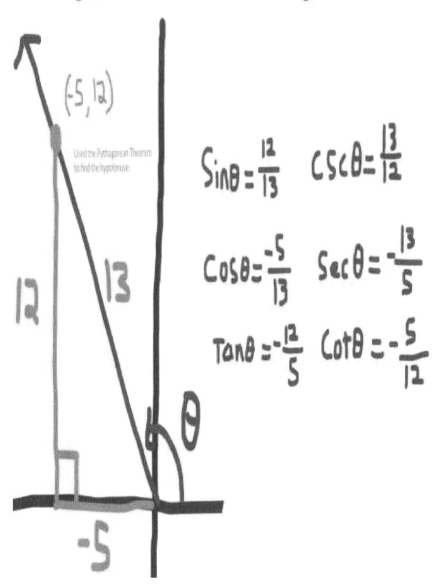

$(-5, 12)$

Used the Pythagorean Theorem to find the hypotenuse.

12

13

-5

θ

$$Sin\theta = \frac{12}{13} \qquad Csc\theta = \frac{13}{12}$$

$$Cos\theta = \frac{-5}{13} \qquad Sec\theta = -\frac{13}{5}$$

$$Tan\theta = -\frac{12}{5} \qquad Cot\theta = -\frac{5}{12}$$

Study Tip 17: Think of Questions to Ask

Asking questions in front of your peers or in a large classroom can make anyone feel uncomfortable. There is always the risk that someone may think your question was dumb, or you just may feel uncomfortable speaking out in large group settings. Unfortunately, having unanswered questions will make it very difficult to understand what is going on. So, the bottom line is you need to ask the question or find some alternative means for getting them answered. When I was in college, I remember how uncomfortable I was at first, but after a while, you get used to asking questions. In fact, others may thank you for asking the questions, because it was one they had.

For math class developing and getting answers to questions is an important part of the learning process. Always attempt every problem in your homework and get help with any problem that gives you trouble. Another reason to listen to other people's questions is that they may have a question that you haven't thought of or gotten to yet.

Unit Circle

A circle of unit radius one
The Unit Circle for trig is fun

Terminal side of an angle goes through
A point on the circle, it's nothing new

Trig values given all around
Points on the circle get you off the ground

x is the cosine, y is the sine
The tangent is y over x all the time

Now angles in multiples of ninety degrees
We'll find trig values, it'll be a breeze

Radian and Degree Angles

Angle of rotation, all the way around
360 degrees, a favorite for the crowd

Radius of a circle, and arc length's measure
When they're equal, a radian is treasured

360 incremental degrees
2 pi radians is equal to these

Multiply the measure by 180 over pi
Converting to degrees, the numerator's why

Pi over 180 gives radians for thee
For the same reason, as far as I can see

Angles of rotation using radians and degrees
Betcha never thought it would be such a breeze

Graph of Sine and Cosine

Periodic functions, called sine and cosine
Learn to graph them, it's done all the time

Unit circle, the parent function's friend
Sine and cosine all around and then

Period of the parent is 360 degrees
Or 2pi radians if you're using these

Divide 2pi by the dilation factor
To find the period of the time benefactor

Half the distance from min to max
Call it amplitude, you need to relax

It's just the number on the outside
Vertical dilation factor, another name coincides

Sinusoidal axis or vertical shift
Synonymous meanings to keep us adrift

Then there's the horizontal phase displacement
Just a translation, no need for amazement

Don't forget the sine and cosine pattern
When doing graphs, it turns on the lantern

Middle-max-middle-min
We call it sine, it's not a sin

Max-middle-min-middle
Cosines in time like playing a fiddle

$$y = 2\sin\big(3(x-30)\big) + 4$$

$$y = 2\cos\big(3(x-30)\big) + 4$$

Amplitude $= 2$

Period $= \dfrac{360}{3} = 120°$

Horizontal Scale $\Rightarrow \dfrac{120}{4} = 30$

Horizontal Shift 30° right

Vertical Shift 4 units up

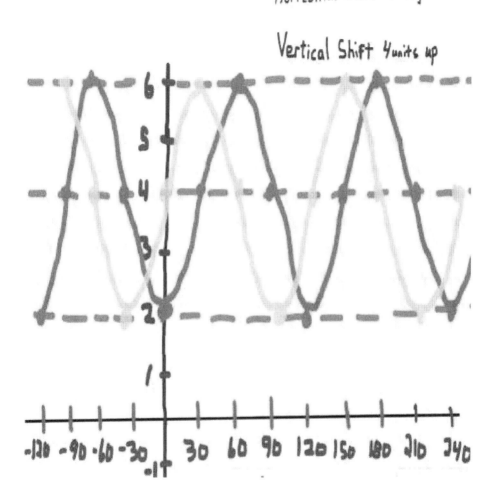

Arc Cosine

Trigonometric models for periodic events
The sine or cosine will help pay the rent

Their sinusoidal graphs contain the answers
Of the events' solutions with no need for dancers

A cosine's inverse's called ArcCosine
For finding solutions, it's done all the time

A cosine's argument is found this verse
It's plus or minus the cosine's inverse

Don't forget our increments of 2 pi
Or 360 degrees, the period is why

Now the variable inside the cosine's argument
When solved algebraically, you've reached the monument

Oh ArcCosine, our trigonometric friend
Solving our problems, so true to the end

Rotary Motion

Angular velocity in radians, not degrees
Just multiply by the radius of the circle now, please

A linear velocity is what we get
Traveling down the road in our car while we sit

Multi-Angle Formulas

Sines and Cosines of angles multiplied
Expressed as functions of single angles classified

The sine of two theta, make this your beta
It equals twice the sine-cosine theta

Cosine 2x, this one is next
Cosine squared minus sine squared in text

1 minus 2 times the sine squared x
or 2 cosine squared minus 1 on the test

The next part of this poem I hate to do
I'm going off on a tangent for you

2 times the tangent, over 1 minus squared tan
Is the tangent of 2x in a double angled plan

$$Sin2\theta = 2Sin\theta Cos\theta$$

$$Cos2\theta = Cos^2\theta - Sin^2\theta$$
$$= 2Cos^2\theta - 1$$
$$or$$
$$= 1 - 2Sin^2\theta$$

$$Tan2\theta = \frac{2Tan\theta}{1 - Tan^2\theta}$$

Study Tip 18: Have Good Attendance

Nothing is as good as being in class prepared and on time. Missing as little as one day a week can lower a student's GPA. There is a strong correlation between attendance and grades. Also, remember study tip 5? How are you going to study your math notes 3-5 minutes before class if you are tardy?

For the last couple of years, I have been posting all my lessons online, so if a student is absent, they can watch the lesson from home. I do have a few absent students who watch the online lessons, and do well on the homework and tests. But the majority of those who are absent do not do very well. Maybe it's because they're not concerned enough to watch the online lessons. Or, maybe there is another reason for not attending class.

First of all, the practice of posting lessons online was always intended as a supplement, not a replacement, to attendance in class. Remember, the more interactions, the deeper the understanding and long-term memory on the subject. Attending class is extremely important; in fact, those who interact with the subject material in the classroom are more likely to remember long-term than those who just watch the lesson online.

Also, being tardy to a class is like getting off on the wrong foot in a journey. Try to be in every class a couple of minutes early with the focus on preparing for the lesson. Get off on the right foot, and complete your journey.

Vectors

A directed line segment, to some it's called
Its length called magnitude for those involved

A mathematical model for force and direction
Or an airplane's velocity with course correction

The tail begins at the head it ends
An arrow indicates the direction, then

Vectors with equal directions and magnitudes
Are all the same, so don't get an attitude

Connect the head to the other's tail
A resultant combination of vectors entail

It's the tail of the first vector to the head of the last
The resultant vector comes out really fast

A scalar multiple of any vector
Changes the length, but not the director

Component form, just plot the point
Then draw the arrow right out of the joint

A unit vector of magnitude one
Just divide by the length and have some fun

With a minus b, when subtracting see
From the head of **b** to head of **a**'s tree

With parallelograms using geometry
a plus **b** is in the diagonal you'll see

Whether combining forces, or the components of wind
Your knowledge of vectors will help us win

Position Vectors

Okay students, assume your positions
The battle begins and were on a mission

An objective to learn position vectors
We will achieve, in learning this sector

On the coordinate system, we fix the tail
At the origin, and off we sail

A position vector is what it's called
Tail at the origin and that's not all

To add or subtract, just combine components
The sum or difference is found at that moment

So time to dig in, move tails to the origin
For position vectors, let the lesson begin

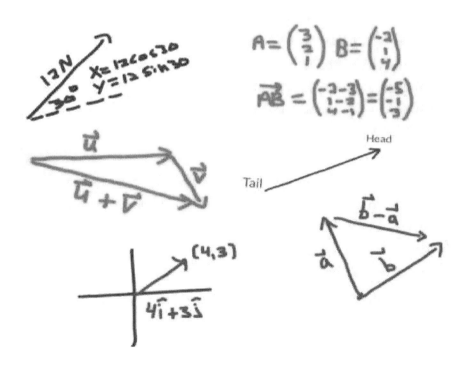

Scalar Product

Back in the day, I'd climb the wall
An expert scalar would not fall

I used to fish, and swim in lakes
But scaling later I could not take

Later a scalar product of vectors
I'd find the angle of a given sector

It's the length of "a" times the magnitude of "b"
Times the cosine of the angle in between

A product of vector corresponding components
A dot product it's called, try once and you'll own it

Whether scaling walls or a catch of fish
Scalar products will grant every wish

Vector Equation of a Line

Please don't crossover, a line is drawn
Respecting boundaries, don't walk on my lawn

A vector equation will help you see
An equation of a line right up to the tree

Subtraction will give the direction to go
We'll start from a point, then off to the show

Lines concurrent, they do intersect
A point in common from the homework set

Slope-intercept equation or vector form
Vector equations of lines are the norm

Study Tip 19: Make Use of Every Minute

Tic toc, tic toc… seconds add to minutes, minutes to hours, and hours to days. Just 5 minutes wasted per day is over an hour in just two weeks, or over 30 hours in a year. Some people waste hours per day. Do they have any idea what those wasted hours add up to? How much more could they have gotten done if they applied those hours to something productive?

Try to think of moments throughout the day where you are not doing anything, like waiting for a bus, riding the light rail, or maybe waiting in a long line somewhere. These are perfect opportunities to go over notes, work on reading assignments, etc. By turning just 30 minutes per day of opportunity time towards study, a student can add 7 hours of study time per two-week period.

Sequences and Series

All ducks in a row, or dominos
They fall in sequence when ready to go

A list of numbers, a particular order
Derived by a rule for the ambitious recorder

Call it a sequence, numbers in line
Finite or infinite, yet right on time

Sum them up, then call it a series
Yes, add them up, you'll see very clearly

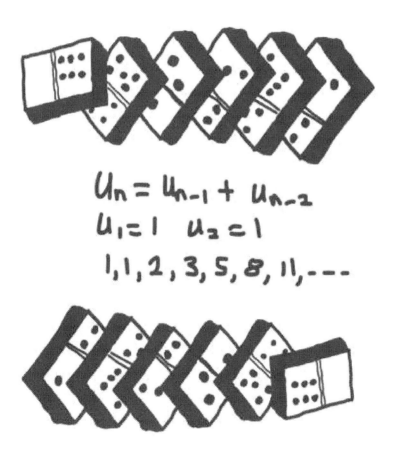

$$U_n = U_{n-1} + U_{n-2}$$
$$U_1 = 1 \quad U_2 = 1$$
$$1, 1, 2, 3, 5, 8, 11, \text{---}$$

Arithmetic Sequences and Series

From term to term, a constant up or down
An arithmetic sequence will turn you around

A constant difference, **d** it's called
Just subtract the term before, that's all

Subtract one from **n** and multiply by **d**
Add the first term, the **nth** one you'll see

Sum them up, a series is fun
It's **n** over two, times the first and last one

Series and sequences arithmetically
From term to term, so beautiful to me

$$U_n = U_1 + (n-1)d$$

$$S_n = \frac{n}{2}(U_1 + U_n)$$

or

$$S_n = \frac{n}{2}(2U_1 + (n-1)d)$$

Ex:

$$3 + 6 + 9 + \cdots + 99$$

$$n = 33 \quad U_1 = 3$$

$$S_{33} = \frac{33}{2}(3+99) = 33(51)$$

$$= \boxed{1683}$$

Geometric Sequences and Series

A constant multiplier to the next term
Geometric sequences, no need for concern

A common ratio, the multiplier is called
Ratio of the term before it involved

An **nth** term formula comes easily
In the next verse, I'll show it to thee

Ratio in common to the **n** minus one power
Multiplied by the first, the **nth** term will flower

Next we sum, now called a series
In the next stanzas, I'll try to speak clearly

One minus **r** to the power of **n**
Divided by one minus **r** in the end

Multiply the result by the first term
Geometric series are not much concern

$$U_n = U_1 r^{n-1}$$

$$S_n = \frac{U_1(1-r^n)}{1-r}$$

$$S_\infty = \frac{U_1}{1-r} \quad 0 < |r| < 1$$

Ex: $3, 6, 12, 24, \ldots$

$U_1 = 3 \quad r = 2 \quad U_5 = 3(2)^{5-1} = 48$

Summation Notation

A series it's called when we add up the terms
The notation for summation is your next concern

The Greek letter Sigma, it's not an enigma
Just the letter S, so let's clear the stigma

S for summation, now we make sense
Let's add up the terms, or pickets in a fence

Just substitute to the expression, where the index begins
Continue the process till you get to the end

Now add up the terms of the sequence involved
With summation notation, a series evolves

$$\sum_{n=1}^{4} n^2 = 1^2 + 2^2 + 3^2 + 4^2 = 30$$

$$\sum_{x=3}^{5} 2x = 2(3) + 2(4) + 2(5) = 24$$

$$\sum_{t=1}^{3} \frac{t+1}{2} = \frac{1+1}{2} + \frac{2+1}{2} + \frac{3+1}{2} = 4\frac{1}{2}$$

Binomial Expansion Theorem

Take a binomial to the power of ten
I'll be back next year, you should be done by then

Expanding binomials of higher powers
Without a theorem may take you hours

Pascal's Triangle carries some clout
It give the coefficients when you work it on out

The triangle's row match the binomials exponent
The numbers in it gives the expansion's coefficients

Many different patterns to the degree of the terms
They equal the power of the binomial concerned

A pattern of ascending and descending exponents
One up, one down for each term in the moment

Get some practice to master these patterns
Like a planet with rings, our sixth planet,
Saturn

General Expression for a Binomial Expansion

$$(x+y)^n = \binom{n}{0}x^n y^0 + \binom{n}{1}x^{n-1}y^1 + \binom{n}{2}x^{n-2}y^2 + \ldots + \binom{n}{n}x^0 y^n$$

Example with Pascals Triangle:

$$1$$
$$1 \quad 1$$
$$1 \quad 2 \quad 1$$
$$1 \quad 3 \quad 3 \quad 1$$
$$1 \quad 4 \quad 6 \quad 4 \quad 1$$
$$1 \quad 5 \quad 10 \quad 10 \quad 5 \quad 1$$
$$\vdots$$

$$(x+y)^4 = 1x^4 + 4x^3 y + 6x^2 y^2 + 4xy^3 + 1y^4$$

137

Spring Break

Winter is over, spring has arrived
The world around now comes back alive

Melting snow, warmth of the sun
Freshness and renewal to each and everyone

Flowers and plants now come in bloom
Permeating the air with lovely perfume

Birds of the morning, give music so gentle
Hearts are warmed by sounds instrumental

Rain will fall, relieving all strife
Nature gets busy bringing forth new life

Students in school, going on break
Breathing a sigh of relief, so great

A time to reflect, a time to ponder
How to spend it, minds will wander

Soon back in school, content and safe
Our next break is summer, we just can't wait

Study Tip 20: Teach another Person

Teachers from all subject areas understand that the teacher always learns more than the student. Anytime you have to break down a concept for another's understanding, your own understanding deepens in a very permanent way. So find a friend or a younger sibling, and teach them your new concepts. Join a study group, and take every opportunity to interact and explain your own reasoning. When in class, participate to the fullest.

When I was in college, while participating in class, I would always look for someone who needed help with a problem. When attempting to help, my own understanding increased. In some cases, I didn't even know how to do the problem before volunteering to explain. The funny thing was that in the process of explaining, I would simultaneously reason it out. By breaking it down for another person, I was actually breaking it down for myself.

Line of Best Fit

Just a plot of ordered pairs
For all the data we have out there

In stats it's called a scatter plot
You'll see a trend, you're getting hot

When points on the scatter show a linear trend
A line of best fit comes in to mend

Points lined up in a positive direction
Correlation of 1 we learn in this section

Sometimes it happens with a downward trend
The correlation is negative, but that's not the end

When points are scattered all over the place
The correlation is zero, no time to waste

So the best fit line is closest to all
It follows the trend of the scatter plots call

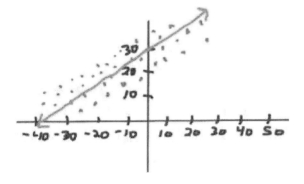

Cumulative Frequency

Just total the frequencies along the table
Yes add them together as you are able

Frequencies accumulate while going along
Cumulative frequencies play such a sweet song

Plot them so nicely along a curve
x-axis with upper class boundaries observe

Vertical axis with frequency totals
Now plot the graph so freely and mobile

Measures of Central Tendency

Central tendencies and measures of Center
At Central High School a statistical treasure

What's the average score on a test?
Just find the mean, I'll tell the rest

Sum the elements in the set
Divide by how many, a mean you get

Order the numbers and find the middle
A median found with no need to twiddle

A favorite food called pie ala mode
The most frequent element we call a mode

At Central High we love the center
A statistical measure for the experimenter

Measures of Dispersion

Is the data close or spread wide apart?
Dispersion measures are a good place to start

Range of values from min to max
Max minus min is a matter of fact

IQR, interquartile-range
Q3 minus Q1 sounds so strange

Variance of data is another cool measure
A standard tool statisticians really treasure

Just square the difference of the data mean pairs
Then divide by sum of the elements in there

When we square root the data's variation
Our measure's now called the standard deviation

For analyzing data, useful in statistics
Dispersion of data is nothing futuristic

$$\text{Range} = \text{Max} - \text{Min}$$

$$\sigma^2 = \frac{(X - \bar{X})^2}{n}$$

$$\text{IQR} = Q_3 - Q_1$$

$$\sigma = \sqrt{\frac{(X - \bar{X})^2}{n}}$$

Box and Whisker's Plots

I put my cat inside a box
A box with whisker's mathematical plot

Min to the max, the whisker's please
The range of data displayed for thee

Q1 to Q3, the width of the box
An IQR is ready to rock

Median is also on display
Inside the box, what can I say?

So whether a cat or list of data
A box with whiskers is coming right at you

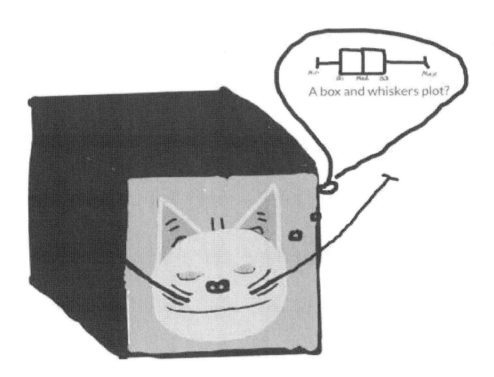

Histograms

With groups of data within class intervals
Histograms are useful and sure the way to go

Placing class intervals on the horizontal axis
It's just the bar's width, no need to attack this

A frequency density gives the height of the bar
Just divide by the width and you'll sure go far

Beautifully displaying, so visually
Histograms for data are something to see

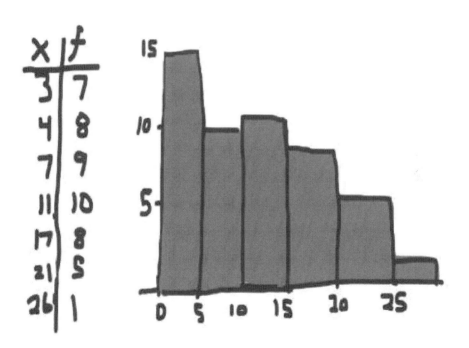

Normal Distribution

Thought we were normal, well think again
We must fall inside the dis-tri-bu-tion

Approximately normal, a bell shaped curve
Mean and median are the middle observe

From one standard deviation of the mean
Sixty-eight percent of the data is seen

From two standard deviations, ninety-five percent
With five percent outside of this tent

From three standard deviations, the majority
Ninety-nine point seven is the percent for thee

For finding percentiles or making an inference
Our normal curve will make the difference

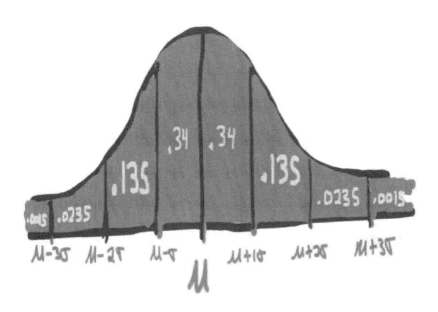

Study Tip 21: Do Every Problem

Jeremy thinks he's good at doing homework, and on any given assignment, he does most of it. On his last assignment, for example, he did 27 out of 30 problems. There were many opportunities to get help on the three missed problems, but 27 out of 30 seemed good enough. In Jeremy's mind, missing a problem here or there, or not completely understanding all the concepts was good enough, as long as he got most of it. Unfortunately, Jeremy failed the upcoming unit test, and he had no understanding why. He did most of the homework, but on the test, it was as if he didn't know anything. So what is going on here?

This is a perfect example of how the small things done on a regular basis can have a significant overall impact. 27 out of 30, or ninety percent, would be a great score on most tests. But most high school math teachers assign homework daily; therefore, 27 out of 30 is the same as missing 3 problems a day; and after 10 days, that's 30 missed problems. It's like going into a test with 30 unanswered questions. Not a recipe for success.

Think of how a slot machine can boast a 97 percent payout rate, yet whoever plays it eventually goes broke. Just use a calculator, type in 10,000, then continually multiply by .97. After seeing how fast your big stack of money goes down, you'll realize that a 97 percent payout is not such a big deal.

Therefore, DO ALL ASSIGNED WORK – 100% of it. Get immediate help with any homework you do not understand.

The Limit

The sky's the limit, we'd like to say
Don't worry, my son, it'll be okay

We limit ourselves in everyday life
While trying to achieve and deal with strife

So time to put our minds to ease
Let's think about limits mathematically

Approaching a number from the left or right
Same function value, a limit is in sight

For continuous functions input the number
Output the limit with nothing to wonder

If the input is not part of the function's domain
Try to rewrite it without going insane

You'll truly know you've hit your limit
When you've reached the sky, with no bounds in it

Limit Properties

Properties of limits are nothing new
If you want, you can learn them, too

Limits of multiples are multiples of limits
Limit of a sum no difference in it

Limit of a quotient is the quotient of the limit
Limits of products, just multiply and win it

So it's time to learn our limit properties
It's nothing new, in math there's lots of these

Study Tip 22: Never Fall Behind

It would be hard to believe you were following the other study tips, especially the important one about working ahead, if you fell behind. In some college courses, getting caught up is almost impossible, because a great deal of work is piled on daily. Therefore, do everything in your power to never fall behind. If you didn't overdo your schedule, you should be able to manage it, and stay caught up and hopefully a little ahead.

If in circumstances beyond your control, you fall behind, talk to each of your teachers about your circumstances, and see if they will assist you in a catch-up plan.

The plan should include doing the most current assignment first, followed by one of the late assignments. The number of late assignments would then equal the approximate number of days it would take to get caught up in the class.

The Derivative

Slope of the tangent to a point on the curve
Taking the derivative will find this, I heard

As points draw closer as one, that's fine
A secant becomes a tangent line

f of x plus **h** minus **f of x**
Divided by **h** gives slope at its best

As **h** becomes smaller, two points become one you see
The slope of the line is at, the point of tangency

Rates of change along the curve
Derivatives will find these, carefully observe

Derivative Rules

To differentiate a function of many terms
Differentiate each one an individual concern

Derivatives of the sums are sums of the derivatives
Same for the differences, you can't get rid of it

A constant function with slope horizontal
A zero derivative is not coincidental

Multiply by a constant, then differentiate the function
Or take the derivative and multiply in conjunction

Derivative of a quotient, a quotient of derivatives
Division by zero is an undefined superlative

Power Rule for Derivatives

A Limit definition for derivatives is cool
But it's so much easier with the power rule

Just multiply the coefficient by the exponent of the term
Subtract one from the exponent, no need for concern

You have the derivative of the given monomial
Applied to each term, you've differentiated a polynomial

$$f'(x) = \lim_{h \to 0} \frac{f(x+h) - f(x)}{h}$$

$$\frac{d}{dx}\left(x^n\right) = n x^{n-1}$$

$$(f \pm g)'(x) = f'(x) \pm g'(x)$$

$$(af(x))' = a f'(x)$$

Undergrad Achievement

Through mental gymnastics, with no acrobatics
You've achieved an outstanding award in mathematics

From normal distributions, worked through some confusion
From quadratic formulas to trig, no illusion

You did some homework and took some tests
You gave it your all and did your best

You set the bar for others to follow
Giving us hope for a better tomorrow

Your parents and teachers, you made them proud
That's why they applaud and clap very loud

Math Mentor Awards

You helped your school, so today we celebrate
You set the example for others to emulate

You listened to instructions and carried out lessons
Your help in the classroom was surely a blessing

You made our school a much better place
You made it an adventure, without the race

So one more thing before we're through
Your teachers and parents are so proud of you

Study Tip 23: Build Yourself Up

A common mistake people make when first entering college is setting a course schedule with too many advanced or difficult classes. The workload becomes too heavy for them to manage, sometimes causing them to drop the program altogether.

Think of a course load to a student, like weights in a gym. Over time we are built up and we can handle more and more. Just entering college is stressful enough; maybe at first you should try just one difficult class with a couple electives and go from there.

Don't overdo your high school schedule, either. If you want to take three AP courses, great, but remember you may have to cancel one of those clubs, or something else, to balance your schedule into something you can manage. Over time, you will become more and more efficient and will be able to manage heavier and heavier loads.

Product Rule

Taking derivatives of products of functions
Multiply together is your first assumption

But no need to multiply, I'll tell you why
We have a product rule to try

f prime **g** plus **f-g** prime
The product rule is right on time

You found the derivative, with no need to multiply
The product rule takes derivatives on the fly

Quotient Rule

A quotient of functions, **f** over **g**
The quotient rule will take the derivative, you'll see

It's **f** prime **g** minus **f-g** prime
Over **g** squared, if you'd be so inclined

Taking the derivative with no need to divide
Quotient rule for derivatives is there by your side

Higher Order Derivatives

Take the derivative over again
You have the second derivative then

Taking the derivative for a third time
You have the third derivative sign

Higher order derivatives, it's all you do
Repeating the derivative and then you're through

Chain Rule

Do your homework, start it now
A ball and chain, it is right how

But just remember persistence prevails
You'll break those chains and set your sails

Today in math we learn a rule
A chain reaction that's really cool

Chain rule for derivatives is what it's called
Derivative of the outside times the inside is all

So break those chains that hold you back
Chain rule for derivatives will help with that

$$(fg)' = f'g + fg'$$

$$(f(g(x)))' = f'(g(x)) \cdot g'(x)$$

$$\left(\frac{f}{g}\right)' = \frac{f'g - fg'}{g^2}$$

Study Tip 24: Use the Internet

For mathematics, you can find a video presentation for almost any lesson ever taught. The internet is a tremendous resource for students of today's era. Just remember that the internet should always be used to supplement, not replace, what happens in class. Nothing replaces good classroom participation. Since the more you interact with new knowledge, the more you own it, it is never good to replace one form of interaction with another. The best thing to do is to combine all the things that you do. Remember, all of the little things add up to the big. All positive things you do on behalf of your learning add together for a big effect on the overall picture.

Exponential Differentiation

Natural log's base to the power of x
An exponential function we differentiate next

Its derivative simply equals itself
Don't overthink and your brain won't melt

Use the chain rule when a function's inside
Derivative of the outside times the inside will fly

Sounds so difficult, differentiating exponentials
Until you try it, there's nothing monumental

Log Differentiation

Feeling distraught, my head's in a fog
Cause our beloved power rule won't work for logs

But that's okay, cause before we're through
A rule for derivatives of natural logs comes true

Just take one over natural logs argument
Derivative is found, we shout from the monument

Don't forget if a function's inside
Apply the chain rule, for an easy ride

Trig Differentiation

Trigonometric functions, sine, cosine, and tangent
Tied for first place at the math beauty pageant

We love these functions, yes we do
We'll take their derivatives on the next cue

Derivative of sine is just the cosine
Cosines derivative is the negative sine

For tangent's derivative, don't be scared
It's equal to the secant squared

Beautifully trigonometric, sine, cosine, tangent
Stealing the show at the math beauty pageant

$$\frac{d}{dx}\left(e^x\right) = e^x \qquad \frac{d}{dx}\left(\sin x\right) = \cos x$$

$$\frac{d}{dx}\left(\ln x\right) = \frac{1}{x} \qquad \frac{d}{dx}\left(\cos x\right) = -\sin x$$

$$\frac{d}{dx}\left(\tan x\right) = \sec^2 x$$

Study Tip 25: Graphing Calculators

Calculators are to mathematicians, as tools are to mechanics. The various features included with most modern calculators allow mathematicians to solve problems that would normally be unsolvable by hand; and without the right tools, a mechanic would encounter many problems that would be unfixable.

Students in high school or college are likely to encounter an occasional math test, and having the proper materials, such as a calculator, sharpened pencil etc., can be an important part of being prepared. Now, imagine a mechanic off to a job, and he has only sixty minutes get the job done. He forgot his tool box at home, so he grabs a random one from the shed. When he gets to the job, he has trouble, because he is not familiar with the tool box – he spends a lot of time looking through it to find the right tools. Now, imagine borrowing someone else's calculator on the way to the ACT exam. Get the idea? There is nothing better than having your own calculator that you have already practiced on.

Critical Numbers

Critical numbers where derivative is zero
Or where undefined, I have to be clear, though

They give the location of the min or the max
Relatively speaking, as a matter of fact

So do not criticize before you can see
Relative extrema on the graph critically

Extreme Values on an Interval

Sometimes we tend to get extreme
When talking mathematics, it's quite the scene

Values on intervals, max or min
Totally extreme as I ever have been

For every closed Interval that ever existed
A min and a max in there subsisted

My favorite relatives max and min
Live on hilltops and valleys within

Reading math poetry is sometimes extreme
Max or mins on the graph are a scream

160

1st Derivative Test

It's the 1st Derivative Test, but please don't fear
We'll find our relative extrema here

Start by finding the critical numbers
Please don't criticize, this test works wonders

Use critical numbers to set up intervals
Across the domain, it's certainly graphical

Derivative goes from positive to negative
My relative max on the hilltops where he lives

Negative to positive, the derivative's tone
Our relative min in the valley makes a home

Derivative the same, on both sides
Neither a max nor a min applies

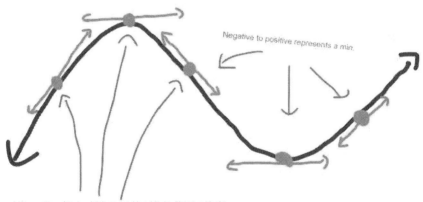

Negative to positive represents a min.

When the slope of the tangent line (derivative) goes from positive to negative, then the critical number is at the local max.

Concavity

Concave down or concave up
It either holds water or pours out of the cup

Use the second derivative to perform a test
For up or down concavity, I'll tell you the rest

Determine the second derivative's roots
A point of inflection may be in cahoots

Roots applied to find the interval
Of concave up or concave down, though

Second derivative a positive number
It's concave up with no need to wonder

Concave down a scary sound
2nd derivative is negative bound

A point of inflection, concavity changes
The 2nd derivative will help you ordain this

So stay tuned next, cause now we're ready
For the 2nd derivative test that rocks so steady

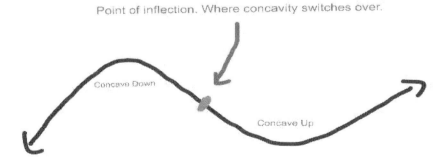

Point of inflection. Where concavity switches over.

Concave Down

Concave Up

2nd Derivative Test

Finding extrema with another test
A 2nd derivative will do its best

Use the 1st derivative, to find critical numbers
Substitute to the 2nd derivative, no wonder

If the 2nd derivative is a negative
A relative max is what it has to give

A relative min, a friend of mine
A positive 2nd is always fine

And when the 2nd derivative is zero
The test, it fails, like Emperor Nero

$$f''(c) > 0 \quad f(c) \text{ is a min.} \qquad f''(c) < 0 \quad f(c) \text{ is a max.}$$

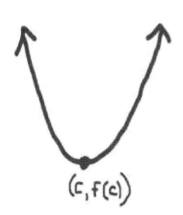

When the second derivative is positive, the graph is concave down, which makes the value at the critical number a minimum.

When the second derivative is negative, the graph is concave up, which makes the value at the critical number a maximum.

Study Tip 26: Learn to Power Read

Reading a textbook for a high school or college course, is not the same as reading a newspaper, or a fiction novel at a coffee shop. If not done properly, hours of time can be wasted. For reading textbooks, you want to learn to power read. Power reading is when you, to your fullest ability, engage the text with all of your body, mind and spirit. Here is a pre-checklist that may help you get started.

- Find a chair that sits upright in an area of low distraction, and a table at comfortable height.
- Read the title of the chapter about to be read, then try to guess, as much as possible, what it is about.
- If there are summary questions at the end of the reading, ponder these before reading.
- Read the chapter summary.
- Read all the subheadings within the chapter, and try to guess what they are about.

Once the checklist is complete, read the chapter while monitoring your comprehension. Monitoring your comprehension is when you pay attention to how well you are understanding and following the text. Since our brain learns to decoded words automatically, a person can go on reading for quite a period, while thinking of other things.

For example, while reading for a class, you notice that you day-dreamed through the last couple pages. The remedy now is to trace back to where you last comprehended. Then, go slightly back from that point, and continue forward. Sort of like two steps forward and one step back.

Highlighting is no longer recommended; what is suggested now is to summarize main points onto post-it notes as you read, and then stick them to the pages where they are on. It may be more work at first, but think of how efficient your weekly review would be when all you have to do is flip the pages reading post-it notes.

Sometimes when reading math-related material, it is normal to read the same page 5 or more times. You would never see a person at a coffee table reading a magazine like this. Power reading is for academic purposes only.

The AntiDerivative

Something over the horizon, I feel it near
It's the Antiderivative, could the end be here?

Our sun is darkened, and the moon blood red
A derivative's nightmare, no resting its head

The book of mathematics, when read aloud
The Antiderivative may deceive the crowd

Our world's derivative, it turns upside down
Integrate the function at the next trumpet sound!

Derivative undone, inverted and departed
Back to the function from whence it started

So don't be deceived, it has other names
Integral & Antiderivative are one in the same

The Definite Integral

To find the area between the curve and x- axis
We need to be definite and precise, like our taxes

Yes I'm definite and absolutely sure
We want that area beneath the curve!

Just take the function's antiderivative
A sketch of the graph makes area intuitive

The Fundamental Theorem finds the area, we'll see
We talk about this next using math poetry

Just integrate the function over the interval
From "**a**" to "**b**" it's nothing personal

Take the antiderivative at "**b**" minus that of "**a**"
It's the Fundamental Theorem, what can I say?

Area is found, most certain and concise
Definite Integrals for area are nice

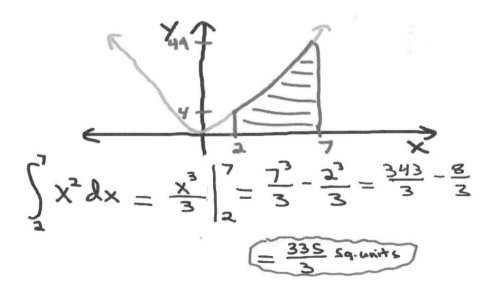

$$\int_2^7 x^2 \, dx = \frac{x^3}{3}\Big|_2^7 = \frac{7^3}{3} - \frac{2^3}{3} = \frac{343}{3} - \frac{8}{3}$$

$$= \frac{335}{3} \text{ Sq. units}$$

Integration of the Exponential Function

The exponential function, **e** to the **x**
Is its own derivative, so what comes next?

An antiderivative, wait and see
Equals itself plus the constant **c**

Now when **e** is raised to a functional power
And the function's derivative is outside the tower

A U substitution is what you'll need
It's antiderivative you'll find, indeed

$$\frac{d}{dx}\left(e^x\right) = e^x$$

$$\int e^x \, dx = e^x + c$$

Study Tip 27: Learn to Power Focus

Related to power reading but in the context of a classroom lesson, to power focus simply means to monitor how well you are paying attention to the lesson without drifting off mentally. To power focus, think mentally in anticipation, like you are getting ready to run a race, and you are anticipating the gun going off. When power focusing, we are in this heightened state of mind during the entire lesson. It takes effort and energy to work your ability to the level of being able to do this throughout the day. But over time, it will get easier.

Integrating One over x

Derivative of the natural log read the text
Gives us the function one over x

An antiderivative, it works in reverse
It gives the function we started with first

So to integrate the function one over x
We're back to the natural log at best

Sometimes useful when integrating this function
When a U substitution is used in conjunction

An antiderivative of one over U
Is the natural log of the function, too

Now back substitute to the variable U
Then add the constant before you're through

Integration by Substitution

A composite function's antiderivative
The chain rule's inverse, so very complicated

A perfect time for a U-substitution
Simplify the integral to avoid confusion

Just let U equal the function's inside
Do the derivative, with dx beside

Now integrate the function with respect to U
Then substitute back and then you're through

A composite's antiderivative by barely trying
With U-substitution, there's no need for crying

Sine and Cosine's Antiderivative

Derivative of the sine equals cosine
An antiderivative we now must find

Take the cosine just for starts
Sine its antiderivative does the part

Cosine's derivative the negative sine
The sine's antiderivative we'll do next time

Negative cosine it sure does equal
It cannot hide if we should seek, though

Trig identities and U substitutions
We'll help avoid all kinds of confusion

Oh sine and cosine's antiderivative
We'll find you out, it's our initiative

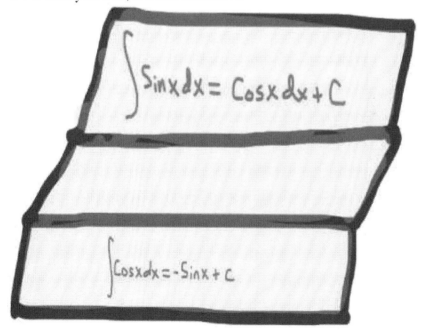

Area Between Curves

Functions continuous, on a closed interval
Area between curves for definite integrals

Between two points of the intersecting curves
One function's higher, ones lower in swerve

Just test a point upon the interval's inside
To find which is higher and which way to ride

Sometimes the graph will help you see
To find the greater one graphically

Take the function above, minus function below
Then find the integral, a sure way to go

The fundamental theorem with limits subbed in
An antiderivative and area within

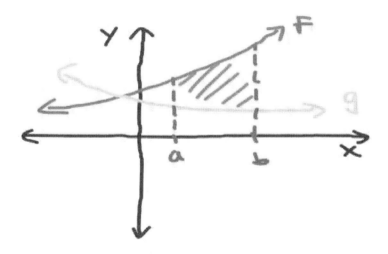

Area between f and g from a to b

$$\int_a^b f(x)dx - \int_a^b g(x)dx = \int_a^b (f-g)(x)\,dx$$

Volume of a Solid of Revolution

With definite integrals we found the area
Next its volume, I don't mean to scare you

Area under curve rotated around
A solid is generated while making no sound

Infinite discs of infinitesimal width
All stacked together, sounds like a myth

Radius of each disc is just f of x
A nice, simple formula I'm telling you next

Just square the function and multiply by pi
Next integrate across the interval applied

The fundamental theorem, a volume of rotation
Precise and accurate, with fancy notation

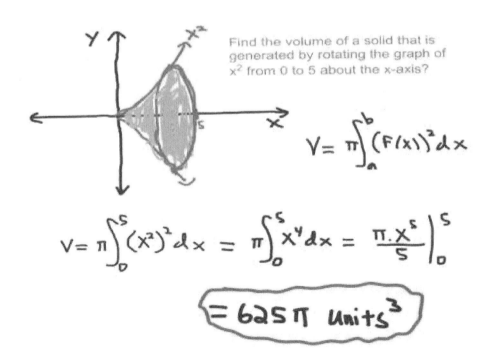

Find the volume of a solid that is generated by rotating the graph of x^2 from 0 to 5 about the x-axis?

$$V = \pi \int_a^b (F(x))^2 \, dx$$

$$V = \pi \int_0^5 (x^2)^2 \, dx = \pi \int_0^5 x^4 \, dx = \frac{\pi \cdot x^5}{5} \Big|_0^5$$

$$= 625\pi \ units^3$$

Study Tip 28: Double-check work

We all make mistakes. On a test, the mistake can simply be a careless one, or maybe we just don't know how to do the problem. Now if you are following all the study tips to this point, it shouldn't be because you don't know how to do the problem. The most common mistake is the careless one. For someone who puts all the preparation time into a test, making a careless mistake can be most frustrating. To have a beautiful test brought down to mediocre because of arithmetic or other simple mistakes, is sad. If given time, simply double-checking all answers will eliminate this problem.

Study Tip 29: Pick a Realistic Schedule

Just remember, you can't do everything at the same time. If you plan on three AP classes next semester, then you may have to cut something else that you like out of the picture in order to make room for the busy schedule. Or if you want to play three sports, work two jobs, etc., you may want to schedule regular non-accelerated classes. If you want to do both, just make sure you are willing to rise to the challenge of the heavy schedule. And be mentally prepared that you may have to give up most, if not all, of your leisure time.

Goodbye Seniors

When your journey began, you were so excited
First day of kindergarten, anticipation ignited

On to first grade, reading and writing
Learning arithmetic, new friends so exciting

It all went by, seemed so fast
Cause now you're a senior, here at last

You learned from friends, teachers and strife
A senior year stressful, yet full of life

Now so ready for next step of the way
Your journey continues, still no time for play

College, military, or getting a job
Or starting a business like the next Steve Jobs

Teachers and friends will say their goodbyes
Wishing you well while trying not to cry

The journey continues, ever onward it's true
Central staff and students wish the best for you

Summer Vacation

Both finite yet infinite life seems to be
Our time in school is like dust in the breeze

We learn to read, write and do mathematics
Classroom discussions, philosophies, and fanatics

Heavy book bags, crowded hallways
Cell phones, iPads, with nothing to say

Teachers and lectures, life lessons and more
Day-dreaming our futures to fight through the bore

Study all night, learning all day
Fighting the urge, we just want to play

September to June, went by so soon
Seemed like forever, or a moment in tune

Summer's now upon us, let's let out a cheer
No more school, time to get out of here

June, July, August, hope it goes slow
Cause coming September, we'll be back on the go

August

Name of a month or month of a name
Augustus Caesar was given the same

Originally named Sextilis in Latin
Sixth of the ten in months we're batting

January and February were added in
Now the eighth month of the Gregorian

A beautiful month, after July
Summer is ending, oh how time flies

Stars in the night, air fresh and crisp
Crickets and critters, a musical mix

Kappa Cygnids, and Perseids
August's the month they come un-hid

Apple orchards begin to open
August's the month where grills are smoking

A name of a month or month of a name
August's the month that ends summer games

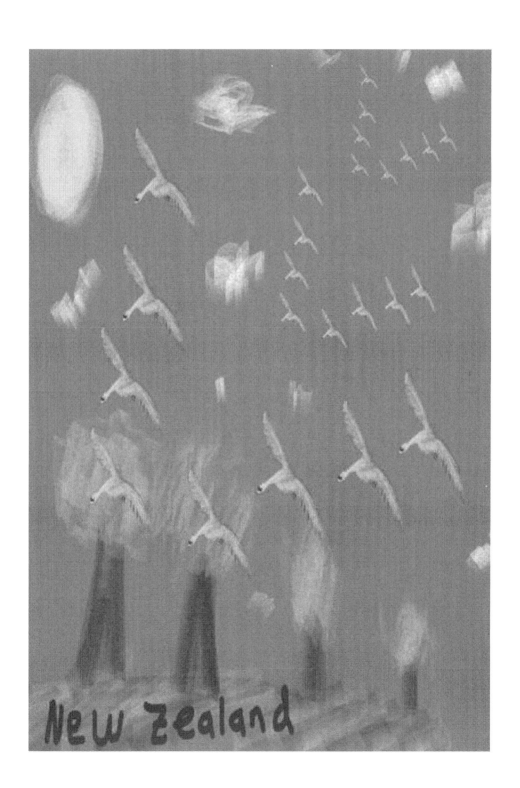

New Zealand

24996259R00109

Printed in Great Britain
by Amazon